M000218080

An Ordinary Life
on an
Extraordinary Journey

CJ Cutaia

An Ordinary Life on an Extraordinary Journey

Trilogy Christian Publishers A Wholly Owned Subsidary of Trinity Broadcasting Network

2442 Michelle Drive Tustin, CA 92780

Copyright © 2022 by CJ Cutaia

Scripture quotations marked AMP are taken from the Amplified® Bible. Copyright © 2015 by The Lockman Foundation. Used by permission. www. Lockman.org. Scripture quotations marked NJB are taken from the New Jerusalem Bible. Copyright© 1985 by Darton, Longman and Todd and Les Editions du Cerf. All rights reserved. Scripture quotations marked NIV are taken from the Holy Bible, New International Version®, NIV®. Copyright © 1973, 1978, 1984, 2011 by Biblica, Inc.TM Used by permission of Zondervan. All rights reserved worldwide. www.zondervan.com. The "NIV" and "New International Version" are trademarks registered in the United States Patent and Trademark Office by Biblica, Inc.TM. Scripture quotations marked NKJV are taken from the New King James Version®. Copyright © 1982 by Thomas Nelson. Used by permission. All rights reserved. Scripture quotations marked NLT are taken from the Holy Bible, New Living Translation, copyright © 1996, 2004, 2015 by Tyndale House Foundation. Used by permission of Tyndale House Publishers, Inc., Carol Stream, Illinois 60188. All rights reserved. Scripture quotations marked NLV are taken from the New Life Version, copyright © 1969 and 2003. Used by permission of Barbour Publishing, Inc., Uhrichsville, Ohio 44683. All rights reserved. Scripture quotations marked TJB are taken from the Jerusalem Bible. Copyright© 1966, 1967, 1968 by Darton, Longmand & Todd LTD and Doubleday and Co. Inc. All rights reserved. Scripture quotations marked TLB are taken from The Living Bible copyright © 1971. Used by permission of Tyndale House Publishers, a Division of Tyndale House Ministries, Carol Stream, Illinois 60188. All rights reserved. Scripture quotations marked KJV are taken from the King James Version of the Bible. Public domain.

No part of this book may be reproduced, stored in a retrieval system, or transmitted by any means without written permission from the author. All rights reserved. Printed in the USA.

Rights Department, 2442 Michelle Drive, Tustin, CA 92780.

Trilogy Christian Publishing/TBN and colophon are trademarks of Trinity Broadcasting Network.

Cover design by: Kristy Swank

For information about special discounts for bulk purchases, please contact

Trilogy Christian Publishing.

Trilogy Disclaimer: The views and content expressed in this book are those of the author and may not necessarily reflect the views and doctrine of Trilogy Christian Publishing or the Trinity Broadcasting Network.

Manufactured in the United States of America

10 9 8 7 6 5 4 3 2 1

Library of Congress Cataloging-in-Publication Data is available.

ISBN: 978-1-68556-717-0

E-ISBN: 978-1-68556-718-7

DEDICATION

I would like to dedicate this book to my husband, Chip, who has loved me and encouraged me to pursue everything that God has laid on my heart for the past forty-two years.

He has been the one who told me to keep writing when it was difficult for me to do so. And fixed the computer each time it wanted to mess with me!

Thank you for your love, support, and dedication to helping me become the woman that God intended for me to be.

ACKNOWLEDGMENTS

Just as in the kingdom of God, we do not go it alone, so it is with this book, and so I would like to thank and acknowledge those who helped along the way.

First and foremost, I would like to say that each of these women that I am about to mention are Christians who love Jesus and are led by Him. Because of His guidance, wisdom, and love in their lives, they have profoundly touched mine.

I would like to thank my mom, who has spent countless hours studying with me, praying over me; together, we have wrestled with scriptures, and she has constantly shown me love and support over the years. As I wrestled over the different chapters, she was the sounding board when I felt stuck on a word or thought.

I would like to thank Pastor Ruthie, who, by the power of the Spirit, spoke to me words that I needed to hear. She advised me to listen to God and take time aside to be healed, rested, and restored. Although she did not comprehend the impact of her words of advice at the time, they were the words that led to the space for God to speak to me about the manuscript I had completed.

I would also like to thank Pastor Rachel for her friendship that was most needed while authoring this book. I also want to thank her for her willingness to read my manuscript with an editor's eye before sending it out to a publisher. She allowed me to expand my thoughts and look at passages from a different perspective. This book would not be complete without her and my mom.

And last but certainly not least, I would like to thank my aunt June and my friends Deb, Doris, and Faith. They have walked through some difficult times with me; we have studied the Word of God together and have served in ministries as friends and co-laborers.

I love you all and am so glad that God has put you in my life to build me up and accomplish His will.

TABLE OF CONTENTS

Preface 8

1. Do Dreams Have Significance? 11
2. Thoughts and Truths I Have Learned 25
3. The Whisper of God; Listening for His Voice 43
4. Time to Return to the Family 57
5. What Can You Do With an Apple? 75
6. Where Does the Apple Come From? 83
7. Where Does Our Spiritual Fruit Come From? 99
8. So How Important Is It That We Have a Good Root Stock? 115
9. Good Soil Needs Good Nutrients 121
10. Seasonal Fruit Growth Has Enemies 135
11. Boundaries Protect 153
12. The Conclusion to the Dream 163
13. The Unseen Enemy 171
14. A Healthy Tree Needs to Be Pruned 181
15. Leading Up to the Battle 187
16. I Have Since Learned a Few Things About Healing For God's Children 197
17. Back to the Pruning... The Second Branch 211
18. Standing on the Promises of God 219
19. The Clock! 229
20. The Conclusion to the Matter! 245

About the Author 248
Endnotes 249

PREFACE

This book took forty years to learn the lessons that I want to share. Along the way, I have learned many truths and experienced many obstacles.

I have also come to realize that I am not alone on my journey. We all have the same lies told to us, misconceptions that we believe, and traps that we fall into.

But Jesus has shown me that He is the Good Shepherd that rescues us, heals us, feeds us, and refreshes us along the journey.

I am also aware that when we isolate ourselves or do not know how to be honest with ourselves and/or others, that is when the enemy is able to do the most harm to us.

I remember when I first started to go to our women's Bible study, I was amazed at how much pain the women were feeling. As I heard their stories, I realized that they were dealing with the same problems and issues that I was facing. And were confused about the same truths that I was wrestling with. We were also looking to the Word of God for answers but were not always understanding the depths of the truths that we were looking into together.

What is discouraging to me is that we don't always understand how God works in our lives or see that the Spirit of God is constantly at work on our behalf. Jesus has paid the price so we can be restored to a relationship with the Godhead, Father, Son, and Spirit. And so, we can be transformed into His likeness by the renewing of our minds through the power of the Word and the Spirit.

My walk with God has led me as a small group Bible study leader to challenge other believers to spend time with Jesus meditating on His Word and letting the Spirit speak truth into our hearts.

And now, I believe, He has led me to put into writing, to share with others, what He has been so gently teaching me about His grace, forgiveness, faithfulness, and truths.

I pray that after reading this book, you will be closer to God in your walk with Him. That you will experience and know without a doubt that you are loved, forgiven, and blessed. This is because you have the Spirit of God living on the inside of you!

Chapter 1

Do Dreams Have Significance?

"The thief does not come except to steal, and to kill, and to destroy. I have come that they may have life and that they may have it more abundantly" (John 10:10, NKJV).

Have you ever had a dream? I am not talking about the kind where you plan your future or even the kind that wakes you in the night and terrifies you because there are snakes under your bed or spiders and bugs crawling on you. If so, those are not what I am talking about; I mean the ones you read about in the Bible. I am speaking of those dreams where you can be awake or asleep, and you say to yourself, "Did that really happen, and what does it mean?"

These dreams or visions have one consistent feature; they are unforgettable, and every detail is so significant that you might feel as though you need to write them down or tell someone so that you do not forget the important parts. If you ever have an occurrence of this type, it should truly impact your life and cause you to see the spiritual world around you in a very real and different way.

Over the years, I have learned that God talks to us in many different ways; the most important to me is the Word of God and a proper understanding of the context. But I have also learned how He works in my life through dreams. And just as with everything else in my life, I did not understand the meaning or application of my first few dreams until after they had come to pass.

A Memorable Dream

I have never forgotten one of my earliest dreams, and it changed the course of my life. It was about marrying a man named Charles.

This dream became my reality in the fall of my first year out of high school.

This is how it began: I was seventeen years old and a senior in high school. I worked part-time after school and on the weekends in the hardware department at a store named Zayre. It is no longer in business, but it was similar to today's Walmart or Target.

While I was working at the store, I met a young man named Chip. He was a construction worker renovating the store. I thought he was ridiculously cute; he was twenty years old and graduated from high school. He had been working at his dad's construction company since he was a teenager and was in line to take over the business when his dad retired. He had his license and drove one of the company's trucks. He seemed to have it all together. He had such an easy-going gentle spirit, with a great sense of humor; I was immediately drawn to him.

The first day I met him, I liked him so much that I went home and said I was going to marry him. He seemed to me to be so different from any of the boys I had known growing up in the "project." He seemed to have his life in order, and it looked as though his future was already planned out for him by his father and the place he held in the company.

My plans were already set in motion as well. All through high school, I had taken classes to prepare for a secretarial job. In my senior year, I had worked in an internship as part of my courses, so I thought I would be looking for a full-time position in an office once I graduated, but God had other plans for both of us, which, at the time, were not known to us. Proverbs 19:21 (NIV) tells us, "Many are the plans in a person's heart, but it is the LORD's purpose that prevails."

There Are Always Twists in the Road

So, in my mind, my newfound love was perfect for me, but again, the best-laid plans do not always fall into place immediately. I soon found out Chip was not as interested in me as I was in him; he liked a girl that also worked at the store.

She was a girl that lived two houses down from me. She was two years older than I and had already graduated high school. She was pretty and shorter than I. I was tall, in fact, taller than Chip. But because of my insecurities at the time, I did not notice. He was bigger than life to me.

She also had a great little figure. I was a beanpole with no distinguishing features. Even my sister, who was nine years my junior, was more endowed than me. So, in my mind, I did not have a lot going for me except the power of persuasion.

To my disappointment, Chip asked me about her. And because we had grown up in the same neighborhood and had been friends, he thought I would help him find out if she liked him and if he should ask her out. Now the right thing to do would be to tell glowing stories about growing up with her as my friend; and how they would be great together, but that is not what I told him. No, instead, I said she was a crybaby, and he would not really want to be with her after a few dates.

In reality, she was not really a crybaby but had been bullied, as was I, by a mutual friend when we were younger.

...Side Note—Everyone Has Been Hurt Somewhere by Someone!

When we were growing up, we did not use the word "bullied," but it was happening all the time. We all thought we had to be strong, or it proved we were as weak as the person chasing us said we were. As we have since learned, we fight or take flight.

She would cry and run into her house, which was convenient for her, as she lived across the driveway from our "friend," who bullied us. I lived a few houses down. I had further to run. Also, I was more like Forrest Gump; I could run and run fast. I would run and hide somewhere in the neighborhood as all my friends would be chasing me, teasing me, and making up songs about me. When I found my hiding place, I would wait as quietly as I could, and when they had all passed by, I would quickly sneak home a different way from where they were headed.

Isn't it strange how the people we call friends are the people who can hurt us the most? We choose friends and put trust in those relationships, so when they are damaged, we also can become damaged. The friend that would chase us and threaten us with words or actions was herself damaged. Her dad was an alcoholic and would abuse his family when he was drinking. They would never know when or how he would hurt them, but I came to know when it had happened because that is when my friend would try to hurt us as well.

So, my choice of words about my friend, although not completely honest, seemed to do the trick. Chip decided not to ask her out but instead asked about another girl. I did not know this second girl well. But her mom worked with me and made it clear that she wanted Chip to date her daughter. I again managed to convince him that this girl was not the best choice either.

The Dream

Now, this is where the story gets interesting. A few months before I started dating this man named Chip, I had a dream of my wedding; and in the dream, I am marrying a man named Charles. I remembered being so happy. I had never dreamt of being married before. Unfortunately, the dream did not consist of many details. I only briefly saw the groom's clean-shaven face; I was walking toward him, and he was facing the man marrying us. When I reached him, I looked at the man marrying us, and he asked Charles if he would take me as his wife. Then I woke up. For clarification, Chip had facial hair when I met him and while we were dating. He didn't shave his face until he asked me to marry him.

After having this dream, I would walk the length of my room between my sister's and my bed, holding anything that would represent flowers. I was practicing going down the aisle to get married. And when it came to the "I do" part in the pretend ceremony, I would be marrying a man named Charles. The feeling of joy stayed with me even after the dream.

But in real life, I liked this man named Chip. So, although I was hoping to get married, I did not understand how it would become my reality. And being the first of this type of dream and not really knowing how to hear from God directly, I really did not know the significance of it. But I practiced walking down the aisle with my fake flowers alone in my bedroom almost every day, but mentally I wanted Chip to ask me for a date.

It took a couple of weeks for him to do so, but when I turned eighteen in June, he asked me to lunch at a carnival next to our store. I did not realize it at the time, but he was waiting for me to turn eighteen before asking me out. He was turning twenty-one in August.

I had officially graduated from high school; it was my first time working a full-time job. It was also the first time I had dated a man, and he had a means of transportation. I had my own money; I could go where I wanted to go and do what I wanted to do. I could be free from my neighborhood and the constant pain that engulfed my spirit.

Dating...

When we started dating, we were both all in, and all summer long, he showed me just how committed he was to our relationship. We would talk at work and have lunch together. During the week, he would come to work in Woburn from Natick. This was about a forty-five-minute drive in good traffic. He would go home at the end of the day to shower and change and get ready to meet me later. He would drive back to pick me up; we would then drive into Boston for a date. At around 10:00 p.m., he would drop me off at home before returning to Natick to do it again the next day. I felt special, and I felt loved.

This went on all summer long. No one had ever shown me this much attention or brought me outside of my neighborhood for a date. We would go into Boston to the North End for the festivals or for dinner and play bocci ball with the old Italians or just eat on the outdoor benches for dinner while we watched people live and work and play. We spent hours talking to each other. I felt like I could tell him anything. But along the way, he kept saying to me, "If you love me..." I later learned that he was just as messed up and insecure as I was, but for different reasons.

And is not it the enemy's tactic to have us chase after that one thing that seems to elude us and for us to allow our emotions to dictate our actions? I believed the lie that said I had to prove my love by giving myself away. I had already had a history of having multiple boys and men try to steal my virginity, but now it came from a different approach. And my weakened spirit just wanted to be accepted. So, with that first night of "lovemaking," my first daughter was conceived.

Is the Dream Dead?

Meanwhile, I still had been thinking about the dream of marrying a man named Charles, but I now thought, well, that dream just died. Because as soon as I told my mom that I missed my period, she told me that I had to tell my dad that I was pregnant. And my dad told me that I had to get married. This was not how I planned to end my first summer after graduating from high school.

But by October, it was decided by my parents that we would be getting married, and I would be moving in with Chip and his family. He did not have his own place at the time. He had been helping out his mom, who was in the middle of a divorce. And everything was happening so quickly that after we got married, I moved into his mom's house with them.

Now the first thing we were told to do was go to the town hall to fill out the marriage license. But before we went, my charming boyfriend did the right thing. He asked me to marry him and put a diamond on my finger. You might think this was not a big deal, but it truly was. Because the enemy was in the background trying his best to destroy this union that God was putting together.

The Enemy's Tactics

I believe the enemy was trying to rob me of my future. My father-in-law to be was not only willing to give Chip a plane ticket to go to Florida and disappear until I had moved on but was, in fact, insisting that Chip not marry me.

I was incredibly angry that I was pregnant. For all those years that I had been victimized by others and wondered where God was in those circumstances, now I was wondering again why this was happening to me. I had excessively big trust issues, and this was not helping.

Everywhere I turned, there was confusion and opinions. And all I knew was that I was having morning sickness, and a life was growing inside of me that I did not want to lose or give up.

God Is the Giver of Life!

You see, I believe we make choices in life, but God gives us life. He knows each one of us by name, and He forms us in our mother's womb. He put this life in me, and I loved that life from the very moment I felt her kicking in my stomach. Similarly, God had put His life in me; I was not recognizing or responding to His life, but it was still in me.

I had asked Jesus into my life when I was a small child. He has said He never leaves us nor forsakes us, although I had not been taught that truth. I had been taught that when we sin, God turns His back on us; I now know that this is not true. But at age eighteen, I thought God had turned His back on me.

I am so grateful that I did not let fear and other's opinion dictate my actions and cause me to end my daughter's life.

As I am sure you can imagine, this was an exceedingly difficult season and an emotionally difficult pregnancy. I was very scared and confused. I felt abandoned and extremely lonely after being sent to live with my husband and his family, whom I did not even know. But I never felt that I was to abandon the life growing in me, and Chip never considered leaving me.

It took me many years to understand the truth of God's faithfulness to His children, but over the last forty years of my life, He has proven repeatedly that He is with us, and we can count on Him.

Some Christians did, and do, point a condemning finger at people like me. But the saddest thing I think is that I had spent my whole life in church, and when I was sent to live with my husband, no one came looking for me. I never got a letter or phone call asking me how I was doing or where I was. I had been involved in a variety of programs and had spent most of my growing-up life in the church, but now I felt so distant from the building and the members I thought were my leaders or friends.

You might ask, "Then why didn't you go to the church?" The truth be told, I did not have my license. I did not have a car, and I did not know how to get there. In fact, I did not even know how to get home for the first few years.

Does God Really Leave Us to Figure Life Out on Our Own?

Looking back, I see the pain that the sin caused in me and the effect of generational sin in our family. I also remember the shame, the rejection, and the loneliness I felt when I was no longer a part of the community of believers. It saddens me that others may feel condemned or abandoned if they have had sin in their lives. I had often wondered where all those leaders and friends were that had been by me when things were going well. I was so young, immature, and broken; I did not know how to reach out for help. I felt that I had no one to give me answers or support. I was also struggling with an idea that Jesus was mad at me and that God was a punishing God who expected perfection and total obedience; otherwise, He would let us fall until we hit rock bottom.

"But God," I love those words! But God is sovereign and knows how to redeem that which is sinful, broken, and lost. Ephesians 2:4–5 (NIV) tells us, "But because of his great love for us, God, who is rich in mercy, made us alive with Christ even when we were dead in transgressions—it is by grace you have been saved." He redeemed me from that life of sin, condemnation, and abandonment.

The Answer… No, God Is For Us, Not Against Us!

I often think of how Jesus paid for our sins so we could have relationships. When we feel all alone, He is present with us. When that finger of condemnation is pointing at us, He is there with mercy. When guilt finds a home in our hearts and minds, He cleanses us and sets us free. And when we have wandered off on our own and gotten stuck in the thorn bushes, He is the Good Shepherd that leaves the ninety-nine and comes to rescue us.

Jeremiah 29:11 (NIV) says, "'For I know the plans I have for you,' declares the LORD, 'plans to prosper you and not to harm you, plans to give you hope and a future.'"

Do you realize that God spoke those words to the prophet Jeremiah for the exiles in Babylon who Nebuchadnezzar had carried off? God had told them that for seventy years, they would be in captivity, but that they should build houses, plant gardens, get married, increase in numbers, and pray to God for the city. God told the exiles to seek peace and prosperity. He also told them not to let the prophets and diviners among them deceive them; because, in His timing, God would gather the people and bring them back from captivity. He said He would bring them back to the place from which He carried them into exile (Jeremiah 29:1–14).

God wants us to turn to Him when we have become captive, and He will be faithful to deliver us in His timing and for His purposes. Jeremiah 29:12–14a goes on to say,

"Then you will call on me and come and pray
to me, and I will listen to you. You will seek
me and find me when you seek me with all
your heart. I will be found by you," declares
the LORD, "and will bring you back from
captivity."

Jeremiah 29:12–14a (NIV)

Psalm 32:8–10 tells us,

I will instruct you and teach you in the way
you should go;
I will counsel you with my loving eye on you.
Do not be like the horse or the mule, which
have no understanding, which must be
controlled by bit and bridle, or they will not
come to you.
Many are the woes of the wicked, but the
LORD's unfailing love surrounds the one who
trusts in him.

Psalm 32:8–10 (NIV)

Spoiler Alert...The Dream Comes to Pass!

Back to the Dream...

So, now it was settled; we were getting married. So off to the town hall we went. As we were filling out the paperwork for our marriage license, I noticed Chip wrote down on the line that asked for his name, "Charles A. Cutaia, Jr." What? I honestly had to ask him why he put that name on the paper. I thought his legal name was Chip Cutaia. It had never dawned on me that it was a nickname. He was the third Charles in his family line, so he received the nickname "Chip." There it was, right in front of me, my dream of marrying a man named Charles was about to become my reality.

My big day had arrived, but it was not as I had practiced in my bedroom. We married on Friday the 13th of October under a full moon. My pastor, whom my family had known for years, did not perform the ceremony. I was married by a complete stranger with a state instituted ceremony. I did not walk down the aisle of our church. I walked into a living room with a dog barking and a phone ringing. I did not wear a beautiful wedding gown. I wore a friend's dress because my dresses did not fit anymore. We had two witnesses, my friend and one of Chip's friends. I tried to put a ring on Chip, but his finger was so swollen that it did not fit. The JP even yelled at us for not taking the ceremony seriously, but I do not think I have ever taken anything more seriously than that night.

After the ceremony, we met our parents at a steak house for dinner. There at the restaurant were Chip's parents with dates, my parents, our two friends/witnesses, and a whole lot of alcohol. It was awkward and not at all a celebration. After dinner, we went back to his mom's house. We went straight to bed. It was a single bed with no extra room to move around in. I faced the wall with my back to my husband and cried myself to sleep.

A New Life Together

We awoke the next day and went to the Cape for our honeymoon. Our life together had begun. Once we were alone, we started to see how much we wanted each other and how much we needed each other. It was a good week!

I think God wants us to think of Him that way, just to love Him and know that He is there for us. Grow with Him and let Him be part of our lives. It will turn out pretty extraordinary.

And we stayed the course. I can honestly say that he is the love of my life. We had a lot of growing up to do and a lot of hurts that needed healing. Mostly though, we needed to learn correct theology about God's grace, forgiveness, and what Jesus did for us on the cross.

And I will admit, there were times when the marriage should have and could have ended, but God put tenacity in me and love for me in Chip. We both walk with Jesus now, and I can proudly say that we've been married for over forty-two years as I author this book.

I have become so aware that God has a way of making things good in His timing. On our twenty-fifth wedding anniversary, I wore a beautiful silver gown with all the trimmings. My daughters were my bridesmaids, my son stood with his dad, and one of our pastors performed the ceremony.

As I walked down the aisle holding my flowers, I saw all of our friends and family that came to celebrate with us. We were not nervous this time, and I did not have any trouble putting the ring on Chip's finger. The new wedding rings fit perfectly. And we thanked God for our lives together and the family He had given us.

And to top the night off, we celebrated with a fun reception that my children planned for us.

Also, Chip still gives me flowers every Friday the 13th. It is funny how most people think that Friday the 13th is supposed to be bad luck, but no day is "jinxed" in the hands of our loving Savior, and it is never too late to enjoy His goodness.

CHAPTER 2

Thoughts and Truths I Have Learned

I love that truth is truth and that when you try to play with truth, it comes back to prove itself. For instance, God is the giver of dreams, and He knows how to make them our reality. I was never taught that we, too, could and would have dreams from God. I grew up in the '60s and '70s and was under the impression that if anyone saw a vision, it was because they were dropping acid or some other hallucinogenic. Or they were from some cult that was taking the Word of God too far.

But in reality, was not that what Peter spoke of when the Spirit of God filled the believers in the upper room on Pentecost? Some of the people that were in the crowds that day thought the disciples were drunk. This was Peter's response to them; Acts 2:15–17 tells us,

These people are not drunk, as you suppose.

It is only nine in the morning! No, this is

what was spoken by the prophet Joel

[Joel 2:28]:

"In the last days, God says, I will pour out my

Spirit on all people. Your sons and daughters

will prophesy, your young men will see

visions, your old men will dream dreams."

Acts 2:15–17 (NIV)

(Hereinafter, brackets added for clarity.)

What I was taught was that the gifts were no longer for today, that they stopped with the apostles. But if Jesus is the same today, yesterday, and forever, then why would His gifts go away?

As I started to grow in the knowledge of God and His Word, I began to question some of the truths that I had been taught. For instance, if Joseph had a dream in the Old Testament, and Joseph, Jesus' earthly dad, had a dream in the New Testament, and John's vision is the Revelation, then why would we not have dreams under the New Covenant? We have the same Spirit living in us, the Spirit of truth.

The sad part to me is, if you do not have a church that believes God is behind visions and dreams, then who do you go to for some understanding? If your church does not think that the Holy Spirit works in our lives as He did throughout the Bible and how He promised to live in us, how can you believe in miracles? I have had many experiences over the years that I have not been able to share with my church friends because, frankly, people look at me as though I have two heads. Fortunately, their reactions do not take away from my experiences with God. It just saddens me that they do not understand how God can and will work in people's lives.

So, if you want to study people with dreams, look at the two Josephs. In Genesis, chapter 37, God gave Joseph of the Old Testament a dream that took years to come forth, and there were many trials that he had to endure. In Matthew 1:18–25, Joseph of the New Testament had a dream, and he married Mary a few months later and raised Jesus as his own. And the book of Revelation is still to be fulfilled. I only understood my dream of marrying a man named Charles was a dream from God after finding out Chip's real name and remembering back.

God Always Has His Purpose in Giving a Dream

I want to make it clear that this was not a fantasy dream… It is not that I secretly knew Chip's name, and that is why I had this dream. No, in fact, I had the dream before I met him. This was a God-given dream to give me hope for the present and kept me going when life got hard and our marriage seemed to be falling apart.

In the King James version of scripture, Proverbs 29:18a tells us, "Where there is no vision, the people perish." The word "perish," according to Strong's Concordance, in Hebrew is "paw-rah," and its implication was that of letting a woman's hair flow out from its covering and being unconstrained in the wind, her hair blowing in all directions.

If you have been in any open vehicle while it is moving, and you or another passenger had long hair, you will understand what is meant here. We have owned several Jeeps over the years, and we would take the top off during the warm months, and as soon as we started driving, if my hair were not in a hair tie or under a hat, it would blow everywhere, especially on my face, blocking my eyes.

I came to realize that sometimes it is not just our actions that need redirecting but also our emotions. My emotions were all over the place, and so were my trust issues. I did not trust God, and I did not trust anyone around me. I could not trust my own decisions. I felt I had done everything wrong up till this point.

I also knew I deserved hell and had been told enough times that I would be going there. When I was younger, I had understood what sin was, but in a childish way. "We all sin and come short of the glory of God." I now understand it in a very real and personal way. Sin kills and destroys, and the enemy of our souls is out to do just that; kill and destroy our lives, our relationships, our peace, and our joy.

Why Does Truth Matter?

Thankfully, this is where Jesus comes into the story. He came to save us and to rescue us from our sins, our mistakes, and our failures. He knew when to step into my life and give me a man who loved me unconditionally. Jesus knew that I needed to be loved and how to provide it. He knew that I had not felt loved beyond my parents' love, and unfortunately, I did not feel they had protected me. They did not even know most of what I had been through or what I was doing as a result. Scripture tells us that "We love him [God] because he first loved us" (1 John 4:19, KJV). I needed to be loved.

I also needed the vision God had given me even more than I knew. I love the faithfulness of God because He is faithful even when we are not. Second Timothy 2:13 (NIV) states, "If we are faithless, he remains faithful, for he cannot disown himself." I just wish I had understood that the dream was for my reality and that God had given it to me to give me a future and a hope.

I would have asked Him what it meant. James 1:5 (NIV) tells us, "If any of you lacks wisdom, you should ask God, who gives generously to all without finding fault, and it will be given to you." I did not know this truth at this point in my life. I believe if I had known, I would have had a ring on my finger before I had a baby in my belly. But again, this is the greatness of our God; He knows our hearts. He knows where we are at and what we need to bring us closer to Him.

I hear so many people testify of the goodness of God and how they did not know He was at work until after the trauma or battle had ended. I have come to see throughout Scripture and in my life that God is always at work on our behalf. He is constantly working to bring hope and truth and assurance to our hearts and minds. He guides and protects us. He does miracles among us and in my family. And many times, we don't see Him at work or sense that He is even there, but He is. He never stops working on behalf of those who call on the name of Jesus. I love it! God is always working on our behalf.

But I am so aware of looking into my past, just how actively the enemy was at chasing me. He was constantly trying to destroy my spiritual life before it ever started. When I was young, there was a twisted truth that I was taught. It was that God was sovereign and controlled everything. It was as though we were puppets on a string without any responsibility for the choices we made. Or if we made bad choices, then they could not be redeemed. And that God was bringing all these bad things into our lives.

Understanding God's Truth Changes Everything

"For it is by grace you have been saved, through faith—and this is not from yourselves, it is the gift of God—not by works, so that no one can boast" (Ephesians 2:8–9, NIV).

I have since come to understand the truth of grace and faith working together. It is His love for us, God's justice satisfied on the cross of Calvary, and the working of His Spirit actively changing us from the inside and providing faith to believe and empowering us to do the work God has ordained for us to do.

I now know that I am responsible to know the truth through the study of the Bible, and when it gets down deep inside me, it will produce belief. Then I can make good and right decisions based on the work of Jesus and His Word. We are changed by the renewing of our minds as we saturate ourselves with the Word of God and let Him have His way in us. That means to stay so close to Jesus so that when His Holy Spirit prompts you to do something or not do something, you can obey.

The influences of my past decisions were leading me far from God. Because of bad teaching or lack of the full teaching, I was afraid of God, even though I was His child already.

It took me a long time to understand the effect our emotions have on our actions. When we let outside influences dictate to us how God sees us, and we react to them and not the truth of the Gospel, we will fall victim to the lies, even as God's children.

I have come to understand the sovereignty of God in this context. God is sovereign, meaning He is supreme over everything. But He has created us in His image and given us free will. We are told in Scripture that we choose life or death; we choose whom we will serve; we choose blessings or curses. And although we have free will, God, in His providence, either allows things to happen, or He steps into our lives and changes our course when necessary so that His plans for our lives are fulfilled and His purposes are accomplished. I believe that is an effective way to define God's sovereignty and providential work in our lives.

We are able to see God's sovereignty and providence clearly in Joseph's, Job's, and Esther's lives. In Joseph's life, we see that what his brothers meant for evil, God used for good. God was in the details, making sure that Joseph landed in the right place at the right time to save not only his family but a nation and many peoples from starvation.

We also see it in Job's life. God and Satan are having a conversation that Job knows nothing about but is suffering the consequences of their discussion and the authority God gives Satan, but in the end, Job's understanding of God is increased, and he sees God in an intimate and personal way. Job now has a deeper, more personal relationship with God, and he is blessed as a result. We also see that God did not cause the calamities in Jobs's life but took the hedge of protection off of Job's life. God knew Job's heart and that he would not curse God and die. God trusted Job.

Esther has no choice in anything that she goes through. She did not choose to be an orphan or a Jew in a strange land. She did not choose to be beautiful so that she would be put in a harem of a king. And she certainly did not decide to be the king's wife. And yet she was able to go to him and tell him that she was one of the people that they were about to try to wipe out. God had been behind the scenes and knew exactly the right time for her to be brought to the kingdom, the palace, and the banquet. The result was that her people were able to defend themselves, and the true enemy was destroyed.

I know all of those stories have faithful characters, but looking at others, you see the other side of the coin. Moses tried to deliver his people by killing an Egyptian. But after a few years in the desert and a conversation with God in a fiery bush, he learned how to follow God's lead and free the children of Israel, just as God said would happen.

Jonah was not faithful, but God put him where he was scheduled to go; he just went with a little different transportation. The result was the people of Nineveh repented, and their lives were spared.

Peter denied Jesus, but he was later sent to help feed Jesus' sheep, the people of God! He was the first to speak boldly to the people that he had feared just a few weeks prior. He very eloquently spoke of Jesus as Messiah and quoted David and Joel. About 3000 people were saved that day. Talk about a turnaround!

God was keeping me and being faithful to me, even though I was not being faithful to Him, even though I was not aware of His presence.

It really saddens me that I was taught so much law and not enough, if any, of the work of grace in my life.

But Romans 2:4 in the Amplified Bible reads,

Or do you have no regard for the wealth of His kindness, tolerance, and patience [in withholding His wrath]? Are you [actually] unaware or ignorant [of the fact] that God's kindness leads you to repentance [that is, to change your inner self, your old way of thinking—seek His purpose for your life]?

Romans 2:4 (AMP)

Does What You Are Taught and Believe Make a Difference?

I wonder what my life would have been like if I had known that I could have relied on God and His Word rather than being angry and mistrusting Him. What if I did not always think I was being punished for immature and bad choices, and if I had understood that God forgave me and remembered my sins no more? And that He was with me in those tough times when people were hurting me. I think I would have lived a different life. I think I would have responded differently to the hard things that came my way. I honestly believe now that I could have made different choices if I had understood the work of the cross. Those truths would have kept me and my future family from a lot of pain.

But those truths were not what my family and I were taught. We were constantly looking at our unrighteousness and "the Law." We were constantly told we were going to hell for our behaviors, so I thought God hated me and had already rejected me.

Romans 12:2 tells us,

Do not conform to the pattern of this world but be transformed by the renewing of your mind. Then you will be able to test and approve what God's will is—his good, pleasing and perfect will.

Romans 12:2 (NIV)

Up to this point in my life, I had not renewed my mind. I had been to church my whole life and knew all the stories, but I had not studied them for myself in a deeper way. I was believing what people told me they thought the Scriptures meant. Most of what I was learning was surface teaching or behavior management.

I later learned that I was not the only one who was struggling with what the Scriptures said about our life after receiving the promised Holy Spirit. Or even what the stories were telling us about God, Jesus, and His love and grace that had become our benefit once we believed on Jesus' finished work on the cross.

Sadly, I have also learned that there are catchphrases or key "Christian" words that are used, but a lot of people do not know what they mean. When you take the time to ask them, they are usually uncomfortable because they think they should know what it means but cannot put it into their own words. This causes many people to become confused and frustrated. It breaks my heart!

There Is Power in Your Words

A few years ago, while studying the Gospels, the Lord showed me that this was exactly how the Scribes and Pharisees had so much power. They interpreted the Law as they saw fit to do so. And it got passed down and exaggerated with each generation.

We, unfortunately, were not taught that it was by the power of the Holy Spirit living in us and that as we read the Word of God and meditated on it, the Spirit would make it alive in us, and faith would be produced, which would change us from the inside out. Then as He prompted us to do or not do something, in our obedience, we would show the evidence of the life that was growing in us.

John 3:16–18 tells us how much God loves us and why He sent Jesus. It reads,

> **For God so loved the world that he gave his one and only Son, that whoever believes in him shall not perish but have eternal life. For God did not send his Son into the world to condemn the world, but to save the world through him. Whoever believes in him is not condemned, but whoever does not believe stands condemned already because they have not believed in the name of God's one and only Son.**
>
> **John 3:16–18 (NIV)**

Again, in Galatians 1:3-4, Paul tells us why Jesus came.

Grace and peace to you from God our Father and the Lord Jesus Christ, who gave himself for our sins to rescue us from the present evil age, and according to the will of our God and Father.

Galatians 1:3-4 (NIV)

We do not go to hell because of our behaviors. But our behaviors can tell us what we believe. Scripture tells us that we will be separated from God if we choose to reject God's Son (the Word come in the flesh), whom He sent and let die for us or on our behalf.

In Acts 16:25-31, we are given an illustration of Paul and Silas living out what they believed and then sharing their faith with the jailor:

About midnight Paul and Silas were praying and singing hymns to God, and the other prisoners were listening to them. Suddenly there was such a violent earthquake that the foundations of the prison were shaken. At once all the prison doors flew open, and everyone's chains came loose. The jailer woke up, and when he saw the prison doors

open, he drew his sword and was about to
kill himself because he thought the prisoners
had escaped. But Paul shouted, "Don't harm
yourself! We are all here!"

The jailer called for lights, rushed in, and
fell trembling before Paul and Silas. He then
brought them out and asked, "Sirs, what
must I do to be saved?"

They replied, "Believe in the Lord Jesus, and
you will be saved—you and your household."

Acts 16:25–31 (NIV)

First John 5:11–13 states,

And this is the testimony: God has given
us eternal life, and this life is in his Son.
Whoever has the Son has life; whoever does
not have the Son of God does not have life.

I write these things to you who believe in
the name of the Son of God so that you may
know that you have eternal life.

1 John 5:11–13 (NIV)

We go to hell because of our belief, or better said, our lack of belief in what Jesus has done for us. Choices matter! Your choices and mine, who and what we want to believe. People feed us what they believe is truth all the time. The question is, will we take the time to find out the truth for ourselves, or do we always want to eat off someone else's plate?

Who Do You Believe?

When we study John, chapter 5, we see who and what testified of Jesus' identity. But we also see that the people of His day were looking in the wrong places for God to be revealed. And because of their unbelief in who Jesus truly was and what He came to do for Israel and mankind as a whole, what they believed is exactly what accused them to the Father.

John 5:45 states,

Do not imagine that I am going to accuse you before the Father: you place your hopes on Moses, and Moses will be your accuser. If you really believed him, you would believe Me too, since it was I that he was writing about; but if you refuse to believe what he wrote, how can you believe what I say?

John 5:45 (TJB)

They did not see Jesus as the sacrificial Lamb that took away the sins of the world. They placed their hopes on the writings of Moses, or the doctrine of Moses, or the law of Moses. They were still trusting in their ability to keep the law apart from the mercy of God and grace through faith in Jesus.

I have since learned that if you want to know God personally, then study the Word personally; otherwise, you are eating from someone else's dish, and you might be getting the parts they do not like with the toppings they have chosen to put on it to make it taste better to them.

Another Lie!

One of the lies that was ingrained in my life and in the lives of a lot of people of my generation was that we needed to show the world our sinless perfection. In other words, we not only had to believe that Jesus died for our sins, but we had to prove by our actions that we were indeed saved by becoming outwardly perfect. I am using the word "proving" to mean we had to look good for others or to other people. I somehow had left out the "Jesus" part of the equation and was trying to be the outwardly perfect person apart from Jesus to prove that I deserved to go to heaven. Oh, and I forgot the part about us never being able to keep the whole law. (Live up to the "perfection" standard.) So once you fail and find yourself continuously messing up, when guilt and shame become your constant companions, eventually you stop trying, or you lie to yourself by saying that you are okay because you look good enough on the outside for others.

My life looked like the Pharisee's, and this is what Jesus had to say about it in Matthew 23:27–28. Jesus said,

Woe to you, teachers of the law and Pharisees, you hypocrites! You are like whitewashed tombs, which look beautiful on the outside but on the inside are full of the bones of the dead and everything unclean. In the same way, on the outside you appear to people as righteous, but on the inside, you are full of hypocrisy and wickedness.

Matthew 23:27–28 (NIV)

The funny thing is you can only live this way for so long, and then your sins find you out. Fortunately, if we are God's children, He does not leave us as whitewashed tombs; but cleanses our insides and gives us a new heart.

Who or What Is Dictating Our Actions?

I genuinely believe I married my husband because God, as our Father, had a plan for us, and we together have fulfilled many promises that God has invited us to take part in. I am so grateful that God does know when to intervene in our lives and bring about good for us. But I also believe that God allowed these circumstances so that I would understand grace in a very personal way and learn to trust Him beyond my five senses and my emotions.

So many of us (Christians) live according to the flesh (our five senses and emotions) and not according to the truth of the Word and the prompting of the Holy Spirit living in us.

According to Romans 8:5,

Those who live according to the flesh have their minds set on what the flesh desires, but those who live in accordance with the Spirit have their minds set on what the Spirit desires.

Romans 8:5 (NIV)

James 1:13–15 goes a little further,

Let no one say when he is tempted, "I am tempted by God"; for God cannot be tempted by evil, nor does He Himself tempt anyone. But each one is tempted when he is drawn away by his own desires and enticed. Then when desire has conceived, it gives birth to sin; and sin, when it is full-grown, brings forth death.

James 1:13–15 (NKJV)

I can honestly say that I was living completely by the flesh and my emotions, where lust had the ability to not only entice me but to draw me away. I also did not even know that the Spirit of God was living in me. I do not think most Christians see or explore the spiritual realm in which we are living as children of God.

We miss out on so much if we think the Christian life is only about behavior modification and do not realize that a loving God is for us and not against us. He does know how and why to direct our decisions and to make even our redeemed mistakes a blessing to others.

I have learned God never sees us as a mistake. Although people may make us feel this way, He never does. Instead, He gives us opportunities to see Him more clearly and love Him more deeply as He cleanses and gives us purpose and dignity.

No matter how you came into this world or what you have done, or no matter what people have done to make you feel valueless, never believe the lie that you are worthless, a mistake, or have no future. We are made in the image of God, and He is always for us.

Psalm 139:13–16 says,

For you created my inmost being;

you knit me together in my mother's womb.

I praise you because I am fearfully and

wonderfully made;

your works are wonderful,

I know that full well.

My frame was not hidden from you, when I

was made in the secret place,

when I was woven together in the depths of

the earth.

Your eyes saw my unformed body;

all the days ordained for me were written in

your book

before one of them came to be.

Psalm 139:13–16 (NIV)

The Bible tells us that God forms us and knows each one of us personally and has a plan for each of our lives, so do not let anyone tell you differently! Our job is to delight ourselves in the Lord, as Psalm 37:4–5a (NIV) tells us,

"Take delight in the LORD, and He will give

you the desires of your heart. Commit thy way

to the Lord, trust in Him."

CHAPTER 3

The Whisper of God; Listening for His Voce

**"I am Yahweh, unrivalled, I have not spoken
in secret in some corner of a darkened land.
I have not said to Jacob's descendants, 'Seek
me in chaos,' I, Yahweh, speak with directness
I express myself with clarity."**

Isaiah 45:19 (NJB)

Have you ever heard the voice of God? Many people would say no, but I do not think they would be correct. I think we all hear it but choose to ignore it or pass it off as our own thoughts or imagination.

There have been times when I wanted to hear loudly and clearly what God was saying to me or what He was instructing me to do next. And what I have found is as I read His word, listened to a sermon, had a conversation with someone, or just prayed and listened, that is when I heard God in my spirit directing my thoughts to line up with His will. It is that quiet thought that makes perfect sense when you hear it. It is that "aha moment" when everything is clear and the answer fixes or corrects the situation without any real effort or pain.

I have spoken already about my sinfulness, the effects of misrepresenting God and His Word, the faithfulness of God, and the work that Jesus accomplished for us. But I did not learn those truths from having a dream of marrying a man with a certain name. In fact, the dream did not transform my life. Unfortunately, I continued on the path that I was living for a few more years, a path that was leading to death, until I heard His whisper.

There was a moment that I heard the voice of God in my spirit so clearly; it was as though He was right there in the room with me. As I mentioned in the first chapter, I was pretty messed up in my thinking, and my behaviors followed.

I was now twenty-two years old, married, and had two children. I was working full-time as manager of a convenience store and took on the weekend shifts. It was early in the morning; the sun had barely come up yet, and the main street and parking lot were still quiet. I always arrived early to stuff the circulars in the Sunday papers.

As I sat on the floor with a broken heart that felt so far from God, a heart that knew it had sinned against God, myself, and my loved ones, a messed-up body that was proving the consequences of that sinful life, and a spirit-filled with fear, regret, and failure, I heard within my spirit these words...

"Why are you sitting on this cold hard floor when you could be in My house worshipping Me?"

I was shocked to hear those words. Fortunately, they were the only words I needed to hear to change my life forever. I heard the truth from somewhere, way down deep inside my spirit.

I somehow knew that the voice I heard was the voice of Jesus. **John 10:27–28 (NKJV) tells us, "My sheep hear My voice, and I know them, and they follow Me. And I give them eternal life, and they shall never perish; neither shall anyone snatch them out of My hand."**

God is faithful to His Word: if He said it, He would make it happen. Recently someone asked me what my favorite verse in the Bible was; I had to think about it for a day or two and then realized that Numbers 23:19 is my verse. It states,

God is not a man, that He should lie,

Nor the son of man, that He should repent.

Has He said, and will He not do?

Or has He spoken, and will He not make it

good?

Numbers 23:19 (NKJV)

From the moment I heard His voice, my life changed. I was able to believe that God still accepted me as His own and that He loved me, that He sent His Son to the cross for my sins, that I was forgiven of all my sins, and that I was truly His child.

I realize that not everyone hears God's voice in the way I am describing, so let me explain it another way. It was a thought that was so loud in my spirit that I could not ignore it. And with it came a joy that I could not explain. It was a connection of Spirit with spirit. I was sensing mercy in action.

When I recognized Jesus' voice, suddenly, all those songs that I learned in Sunday school came rushing back to my memory; all at once, I felt a joy that I had never experienced before. Something had changed on the inside of me, and I was very aware that something was taking place in my heart. I felt as though there were strong hands on my shoulders, turning me around 180 degrees.

It is true that, once I left my mom's house, I became aware that I was making my own choices now and that I was responsible for my actions. I had no excuses to fall back on. But the truth was, I was not making good ones and I was very aware that they were damaging to myself, my family, and my relationship with God. And worse was that I kept trying to change myself. I kept trying to make things right by my own power. I was trying to prove to God that I could be good and do what was right.

We, as humans, are a funny lot. We can read things and hear things about God, but until we meet Him personally, we do not understand Him or His ways. We are dead in our sins and trespasses. That is one of the consequences that took place in the garden. Our spiritual connection with God was severed. We hid from Him instead of running to Him.

But when I heard those words, I realized that God loved me despite me. I realized that He had not left me nor forsaken me, even though I had left Him a long time before this moment. So, thank God that we can trust His word that tells us that He loves us with an everlasting love, and therefore, He continues in His faithfulness to us.

Tears of joy will stream down their faces,

and I will lead them home with great care.

They will walk beside quiet streams

and on smooth paths where they will not

stumble.

Jeremiah 31:9a (NLT)

I was finally starting to see and enter into the life that Christ has died to give me, the living hope that He had purchased for me to experience. First Peter 1:2–3 and Ephesians 2:4–5 explain it best.

Who have been chosen according to the

foreknowledge of God the Father, through

the sanctifying work of the Spirit, to be
obedient to Jesus Christ and sprinkled with
His blood: Grace and peace be yours in
abundance.
Praise be to the God and Father of our Lord
Jesus Christ! In his great mercy he has given
us new birth into a living hope through the
resurrection of Jesus Christ from the dead,
and into an inheritance that can never perish,
spoil or fade.

1 Peter 1:2–4a (NIV)

But because of his great love for us, God,
who is rich in mercy,
made us alive with Christ even when we were
dead in
transgressions—it is by grace you have been
saved.

Ephesians 2:4–5 (NIV)

That day I gave my notice at work and started a new adventure. Within two weeks, I was able to quit smoking and drinking, along with other habits I had picked up along the way. I can honestly admit that I had been trying to stop these activities but had not been able to do so. I was beginning to see faith and grace coming together, although I did not know it at the time.

Before quitting my position, I remember walking around the store every fifteen minutes to a half hour, taking the temperatures of the refrigerators and freezers. My usual routine would be to go outside the store to have a cigarette after taking the temperatures, but now I was able to tell myself that I could postpone it for the next fifteen minutes. Fifteen minutes turned into a half hour, which turned into an hour until I found myself free from the habit.

The ability to quit smoking was the work of God. As I had stated earlier, I had been trying to quit on my own for several years and was not able to; now, it was easy and natural.

God Knows How to Seal the Deal

The next thing that happened was amazing to me at the time, but now I realize it was just God's way of making sure that I clearly understood what He was saying to me. I was at home the following day. I walked into my bedroom and saw the television was on. I had not turned it on, and I did not know who had. There was no sound; I did not even see a person on the screen, but there, in bold black letters, were two Bible verses starring me in the face.

It was John 3:16–17:

For God so loved the world, that he gave

his only begotten Son, that whosoever believeth in him should not perish, but have everlasting life. For God sent not his Son into the world to condemn the world; but that the world through him might be saved.

John 3:16–17 (KJV)

I kid you not; I thought it was a message straight from God for me personally. I did not know that there was such a thing as Christian programming. And I was so overwhelmed by seeing this verse, again thinking this was a miracle from God personally for me, that I turned off the TV, fell to the ground, and cried. At that moment, I confessed all of my sins and told Jesus that my life was His to have; I had destroyed it, but if He thought He could do anything with it, well, then it was His to have.

Since my experience, I have heard of many other people who God has touched in a similar way. They hear a preacher say, "I'm speaking to you," as soon as they turn on the TV. Or they see a verse in an unexpected place exactly when they are able to receive it.

I would like to mention that I was already a child of God, but I had lost my way as difficulties came and as I was taught and believed that God had rejected me because of my sinful behaviors. But now, I was ready to receive healing and redemption. I had been crying out for it. I had been trying to fill that hole in my heart that was reserved for Jesus alone. Time and time again, my efforts fell short of my expectations, and my desires drove me away from those I wanted to love and was responsible to care for. But God was at work, and I could see His hand of mercy and hear His voice of peace, forgiveness, and love.

Now I also realize that not everyone has an experience as dramatic as mine. But I do believe that at different points in your life, you will have a personal revelation of Jesus and a realization that you need His forgiveness and that He has already provided it for you through His death and resurrection.

The Transformation Begins

After this encounter of hearing the Spirit and realizing that Jesus loved me, the true journey of transformation started to take place in my heart and life. Now you might think that I ran back to church or to my parents or old friends, but I did not. I spent the next three years praying, studying the Word, and fasting. I ate up and drank in the Word of God.

I lost all of my friends. My body craved things that I was now denying, my emotions were really messed up, and I had severe headaches. I had to be healed, really healed from head to toe. I needed truth, and I needed it from the Master Himself.

I drank in the love that God was extending to me, and I wrestled with Scriptures and truths that I had been taught growing up. I was now starting my journey to an extraordinary life.

I began listening to the voice inside my spirit. I started to renew my mind. I wrote in notebooks; I apologized to people; I lived and acted differently. I was made fun of by friends, neighbors, and some family members. I was now "Saint Cindy."

I no longer fit into the crowd, and that was okay. I was in the presence of God daily, and He was speaking to me through His Word. I was beginning to see things differently, and I was getting stronger in my faith and in the knowledge of how grace had been bestowed to me. I was now aware that I was a true child of God, and no one could take that from me.

It is funny because the Lord told me that His grace was sufficient, but at the time, I did not know what true grace really looked like. I did not know of all the provisions that He had purchased on the cross for me. I did not understand the power that now lived in me, which was the Holy Spirit. I did not know that it was unconditional love that would be lavished on me. I did not understand that God was not mad at me. He had taken all of the anger that should have been placed on me, and instead, Jesus took it on Himself, along with sickness and the curse. I was now living in God's love and the power of the Holy Spirit but did not fully understand what was taking place or how God viewed me.

Leave Your Past Behind

But I did start to leave my past behind me and to remember my sins no more. I figured if God could do that with my sins, and Jesus paid such a price to have them removed from me, then I should have the same attitude and actions as God.

"For I will forgive their wickedness and will remember their sins no more" (Hebrews 8:12, NIV).

Prior to this revelation, I remember waking up each morning rehearsing my past sins and pain. But one day, God told me that I was a new creation and that I was not to wake up thinking on those negative thoughts but instead start my day by listening to a message or studying His Word.

Obedience is such a great companion to wisdom. **James 1:22 (NIV)** tells us, "Do not merely listen to the word, and so deceive yourselves. Do what it says." Because of obedience, I was able to see Jesus' righteousness instead of my sin and failure. Now my joy was continuing to rise up inside me. I still had a long way to go, but at least I was moving forward and no longer looking back.

I was now starting to see the value of knowing God personally. I now craved the Word of God, and I loved when I found a new nugget of truth that sent such joy through my spirit. It was better than any drug or drink I had ever had. And it did not hurt me; in fact, it was healing me both physically and emotionally.

During this time, I had another dream; I called it......

A Place of Hope

In the dream, there was a young woman. She was sitting in a crouched position in what appeared to be a hollowed stone crevice. Starring at her, I noticed that she could not move at all, and she appeared to be extremely uncomfortable. All at once, a sensation of confusion and a wave of terror washed over me. Not being able to take my eyes off her, my mind searched for a reason as to how she got there and why she stayed there.

Then my mind's eye widened as I realized that she was near the top of a large mountain. It was as though one side had been removed. Instead of a jagged rocky surface, there were many hollowed-out spaces. Each one was occupied by a different person, and each person had the same expression on his or her face.

Below, I could hear a loud rushing of water that was strong, almost violent. It had direction and a sense of purpose. I could hear it call to me. Looking down, I suddenly realized that I was the girl in the crevice sitting like a caged bird, yet nothing held me. There were no bars, nor windows, nor chains, just terror.

I tried to call to the others for strength and comfort. The only response, however, was the sound of the water below and the quiet, gentle voice that seemed to come from within me. It kept saying, "Jump into the water, do not be afraid. I will be with you."

At first, my response was: "No, it's too high; the water will drown me." Again, the voice said, "Do not be afraid; I will guide you." Although the voice was slightly familiar, how could I trust it? I made the mistake of looking into the water, thus seeing the rushing turbulent waves hitting against the shore. There were sharp rocks sticking out of the water, forming peaks and swirling pools moving along swiftly with the current.

Desperately my eyes were searching to see who was speaking, but there was no one in sight. But as I lifted my face, a brightness appeared, and the voice again spoke. This time, the words that my heart heard were, "I am the Way the Truth and the Life."

All at once, my heart leaped for joy as I realized with whom I had been speaking. With a sudden burst of effort, I plunged into the air and started falling the great distance into the river below. Unfortunately, the fear had not completely subsided as I had hoped it would.

And as my body hit the water, I became aware of the strong current, the cold temperature, and the fact that I was being carried toward a large iron gate. Again, there was a voice, but it came from outside of me. It was sadistic and mean, and there was a shrill of laughter in this voice. He told me that I was too weak to escape. Panicking and starting to go under, I was overwhelmed with the thought of not being able to escape the powers that held me a prisoner. The realization of why I had not attempted to jump before was evident. I had seen others fail in their attempt to save themselves.

However, I wondered, could I trust the One who had given me the courage to jump? Would the Savior really be able to lift me from the deep? Could He remove the iron gate that lay ahead? Would He give up due to my cries of pain and woe? Would He leave me there to drown in my own self-pity? The place of exhaustion and death was coming even closer.

Then I noticed there was a man on the shore. His face was kind and gentle. His right hand was held out to me. He stood firm and strong. His eyes longed to connect with mine; His voice said that I needed to trust Him. I closed my eyes, lifted my hands, and said in a quiet voice, "I am ready to trust you." The instant the words were uttered from my lips, I felt the grip that restored me to dry ground, opened that iron gate, and brought me freedom.

I thanked my Savior for rescuing me. I sat and spoke with Him for a while. His words brought correction to my life. He gave me strength and courage to go on. He set my feet in a new direction. He gave me meaning and purpose to my life.

I have never gone back to the perch on the mountain, but often when I feel too fearful to move forward and take that leap of faith or see the iron gate and hear the rushing water, I remember God said, "Fear not, I am with you always, even to the end of the age" (Matthew 28:20, NKJV).

I hope you know how loved you are by God. I hope you know that nothing can separate you from His love. I hope you know that He is standing by, waiting for you to let go and trust Him.

Romans 8:31–39 in the New Living Translation states,

What shall we say about such wonderful
things as these? If God is for us, who can
ever be against us? Since he did not spare
even his own Son but gave him up for us all,
won't he also give us everything else? Who
dares accuse us whom God has chosen for his
own? No one—for God himself has given us
right standing with himself. Who then will
condemn us? No one—for Christ Jesus died
for us and was raised to life for us, and he is
sitting in the place of honor at God's right
hand, pleading for us.

Can anything ever separate us from Christ's
love? Does it mean he no longer loves us if we
have trouble or calamity, or are persecuted,
or hungry, or destitute, or in danger, or
threatened with death? (As the Scriptures say,
"For your sake we are killed every day; we are
being slaughtered like sheep.") No, despite

all these things, overwhelming victory is ours
through Christ, who loved us.
And I am convinced that nothing can ever
separate us from God's love. Neither death
nor life, neither angels nor demons, neither
our fears for today nor our worries for
tomorrow—not even the powers of hell can
separate us from God's love.
No power in the sky above or in the earth
below—indeed, nothing in all creation will
ever be able to separate us from the love of
God that is revealed in Christ Jesus our Lord.

Romans 8:31–39 (NLT)

CHAPTER 4

Time to Return to the Family

After the third year at home studying alone, I felt that God was telling me to start to go to church again. But when I went back, I realized I had a different perspective from those around me. I no longer believed that God was always mad at me. I also realized that God put all of His anger on Jesus and that my past, present, and future sins were paid for on the cross. Why or how could God be mad at me if His Son had paid the penalty I owed?

I now know we are or should be motivated by the Spirit working in us as we renew our minds and understand what Jesus has done for us. We cannot understand spiritual truths without God removing the blindness and giving us ears to hear, eyes to see, and a pliable heart that He can write His law of love on.

Ezekiel 36:24–27 says,

For I will take you from among the nations, gather you out of all countries, and bring you into your own land. Then I will sprinkle clean water on you, and you shall be clean; I will cleanse you from all your filthiness and from all your idols. I will give you a new heart and put a new spirit within you; I will take the

**heart of stone out of your flesh and give you a
heart of flesh. I will put My Spirit within you
and cause you to walk in My statutes, and you
will keep My judgments and do them.**

Ezekiel 36:24–27 (NKJV)

These next two poems speak of where my heart was prior to Jesus speaking to me. That is why the verses mentioned above are so beautiful to me. I had that heart of stone. Each time I was hurt by someone or I personally sinned, my heart became angrier, harder, and darker. It was so full of fear and disappointment until Jesus whispered truth to me.

"Images"

Images shift,
Faces change,
Moods swing,
Nothing is the same
Empty promises,
Sorrowful faces,
Disillusionment appears,
In the strangest places
Instant rush,
Created by,
Heightened crush,
Leads to false trust.
Image no longer pure,
Immaturity has scored,
Courage lacks,
Unfaithfulness is back.

CJ Cutaia

"Broken"

My eyes grow weary.
As I look upon your broken bodies
My tears touch the ground.
As I see fatalities all around
Emptiness, loneliness
A mother's heart breaks.
Sadness, shamefulness
A father's heart aches.
Moments of truth
Moments of splendor
Cannot erase the pain.
That your flesh remembers
You are living yet dead.
You are alive but so afraid.
You chose a high
That will always pass away.

CJ Cutaia

Forgiveness Is a Powerful Tool

Along with forgiving ourselves, sometimes we need to learn how to forgive others who have hurt us, whether they realize it or not. This I learned from a pastor at the beginning of my journey. He taught me how to forgive even when others do not want to take responsibility for their actions or, because of their own blindness, are unable to forgive.

And because of this new perspective, I was no longer looking at people the same way. I was convinced that God could find His way into anyone's life who was really looking for Him. I was that lost sheep that He left the ninety-nine to go and find.

The truth is that He is not looking at outward behaviors but instead at our hearts. And He knows how to find and bring back those who are His. This new reality was freeing, although I have to say that there have been a few instances later in my life that took a lot of courage and grace from God to overcome and truly forgive. (More on that chapter of my life later in the book.)

Hearing God Directly

I was also listening differently. I wanted to hear God's opinion above any other voice. I remember being frustrated as I heard church people talk about others who were so sinful and were going to hell because of their behaviors, never realizing that we all have sinned and come short of the glory of God. (Sometimes, I think we look at that verse and think, "They are sinners." But the truth is we all still fall short, but it is our faith in Jesus that saves us.)

I soon found out how important it was to hear from God directly. One example was when I went to a missionary conference at my church. For those of you who may not be familiar with those words, a missionary conference is when missionaries come home from their places of ministry, give reports to the church, and raise money to go back and serve further.

While I was at this conference, I spoke to a few missionaries, and I told them what God was doing in my life and the home in which I was living. They told me that I was too spiritually immature to be living around those people and that I should move out immediately. For some clarification, Chip's family was far from the Lord, and there were situations that warranted concern.

So, after leaving the conference, I prayed about what they had told me. To my surprise, the Lord did not tell me to move my family out of the house, but instead, He asked me, "Did I tell you to move?" My answer was no. This was one of many times when the Spirit spoke from inside my spirit and directed me according to His will and not man's.

The Lord was teaching me to trust Him and His voice, not the voice of others who thought they knew God's will for my life. As it turns out, we did not move out, but the other family members eventually did, and we built another house on the main house for Chip's mom to live in. We own both houses now.

The Lemon Law

Another way He taught me to hear His voice was by what I call "the lemon law." One day I was in the grocery store, and I walked by the lemons; as I did, I had the thought to buy some. I ignored the thought because I had a list, and I knew what I had planned for meals that week and what fruits and vegetables I needed for each meal. (I am a list person; I am well organized and make my list and check it twice.) The lemons were not on my list.

Later that week, my mom called and asked about coming over for dinner. I said sure and asked what she wanted me to make. Would not you know it, I needed the lemons. God knew what I needed before I needed it, and He was trying to let me know, but I pushed it off as just a needless thought. I did not understand at the time that God is in the details. He wants to be part of every area of our life, even the small details such as a simple dinner plan.

This lesson also taught me that if we can hear God's whisper and believe what He is speaking to us through that prompting in the small things, then we can be trusted in larger adventures, and we can trust God to be faithful to us in return. Once we genuinely believe that it is God, then it is so easy and natural to obey. Later in life, when I was catering or planning a large event, I learned to ask God what I needed and how much I needed before going to the store. When I listened, I always had what I needed and the amount that I needed.

What Is in the Box? ...Hopefully, Not God!

The third thing He began to teach me was not to put Him in a box. What I mean by this is to let Him be God and do what He wants, the way He wants to do it, and in the timing that He knows is best. This is still difficult for me, especially the timing part.

There were so many things that I was taught about God that just were not true about His character. We think we know God just because we read a story about Him or someone gives their testimony, but I have learned, and am still learning, that God is so much bigger, wiser, and stronger than we are. We cannot comprehend the plans He has for us. Also, we will never fulfill His plan if we do not let Him out of the box, so we can watch Him work in our lives and we in conjunction with Him.

Here is an example of how God works, even if we do not understand what He is doing at the time. We had the opportunity to be given $20,000 to buy a condo and move out of the house we were renting. It looked like a sound investment and a great opportunity. But as I thought about it, I had a very uneasy feeling and thought that something was not right about the decision. So, after praying about it, my husband and I decided against the money and the move.

At the time, it seemed dumb not to take advantage of the opportunity provided to us. But a few years later, we were incredibly relieved we had not moved when we learned that there was some sexual misbehavior amongst the children in the neighborhood. My children could have been affected, and I was so thankful that we were not involved. (I had grown up with several situations that harmed me in this area.) Later, when the others were ready to sell their condos, they found that they had lost value and that they not only had to pay the bank the difference, but they had to pay the $20,000 back to the investor.

Another time, we were interested in buying a house close to where Chip was working. The deal did not take place, and again a few years later, we read of a very disturbing incident in the neighborhood and possibly the house we were looking to buy. There was a random shooting, and a bullet went through a window, killing the person in the house.

The house we own and have lived in for the past forty years, give or take a few apartments before purchasing the house, has been used by the Lord. We have had foster children live with us. We have had Bible studies. We have had a Christian day care. We have had weddings and neighborhood parties. We have had friends stay with us. Also, the value of our house has increased many times over what we paid for it. You get the picture; God knew where we were to live and why He wanted us to stay put, even though the opportunities that came our way seemed good in everyone's eyes.

I am so thankful that we were able to hear and respond in these situations because we stayed close to the Lord, asked what His will was in each situation, knowing that we could not and should not do anything of real significance apart from Him.

Praise and Worship

One of my favorite songs is "Just a Closer Walk with Thee." These are the words to this simple song:

"I am weak, but Thou art strong,

Jesus, keep me from all wrong,

I'll be satisfied as long

As I walk close to Thee.

Just a closer walk with Thee,

Grant it, Jesus is my plea,

Daily walking close to Thee,

Let it be, dear Lord, let it be."

"Just a Closer Walk with Thee"

I remember singing that song over and over daily. I had seen what life apart from Jesus looked like, and I did not want to live that way anymore. To walk close to Jesus was my one desire and still is. I think the most important truth that God has taught me and continues to teach me and remind me of is the importance of praise and worship.

I think this becomes very natural for us as we walk with God and see His goodness and faithfulness to us daily.

As I mentioned, the Lord asked me the question: "Why are you sitting on this cold hard floor when you could be in My house worshipping Me?" Praise and worship go hand and hand but are not necessarily the same thing. I can praise God with my lips, but my heart can be far from Him. Matthew 15:8 (NIV) tells us, "These people honor me with their lips, but their hearts are far from me."

And Isaiah 29:13 makes it even clearer when he writes,

The Lord says: "These people come near to me with their mouth and honor me with their lips, but their hearts are far from me. Their worship of me is based on merely human rules they have been taught."

Isaiah 29:13 (NIV)

Before meeting Jesus at the store, I now realized that God did not have my heart. I could sit in church and sing songs all day long. I could recite stories; I could even pray in front of my small groups. I looked like the perfect little Christian girl. But on the inside, I had so many questions and so much pain; I never understood how the Bible and my life fit together. I did not understand, at that point in my life, the pain that Jesus suffered for my sin, my redemption, my wholeness.

To understand the power of the resurrection, you must be willing to look into the pain that Jesus suffered for you and me, and you must come to the deep heartfelt understanding that He did it for you personally. Then and only then can you worship in spirit and in truth.

I Wanted to Know the Power of His Resurrection in My Life...

So, I cried out to God for understanding of what the power of the resurrection looked like in our lives. At the time, everything in our family seemed to be going wrong, even though I was going to church and studying the word. The children were always sick, my husband would be laid off every few years, the appliances kept breaking, and we did not have the means to fix them.

Finally, I stopped and asked God the question directly: "If I cannot see any evidence of You working in my life here on earth, then how can I believe that it will be any different in heaven?" Please do not misunderstand what I was asking; I was not asking if God was real, if He existed, or if He loved me. I was asking for the manifestation in my life, to see His Spirit at work in tangible ways.

The beauty of Jesus is He is always prepared with an answer, and it usually comes in the form of a question. But not this time; this time, I was allowed to have a clear picture of where God was working during my years of struggle and pain. I was in my shower singing when the words "Faithful" and "True" came to my mind. Immediately the Lord reminded me of all the hard situations I had been in and all the times I had been victimized as a young girl, and how He had either protected me from greater harm or delivered me from them. I came out of my shower, realizing that no one could ever take that truth from me.

Jesus Is Faithful and True

Revelation 19:11 (KJV) says, "And I saw heaven opened, and

behold a white horse; and he that sat upon him was called Faithful and True, and in righteousness he doth judge and make war." I realized that He had been my protector all along my journey. I just did not see Him because I was so focused on the distractions and pain.

The question that He asks is: "Will you worship Me in spirit and in truth when things are difficult?" It has really benefitted me to realize that when we keep our eyes on Jesus and remember who He is and what He has done for us, and worship Him at all times, then we will have peace and joy.

I have come out of my shower more times than I can count with a different perspective from when I went in. It is not that the situation has changed, but it is because I have gone to the throne of grace with my questions, hurts, pains, and confusion. He has been Faithful and True to hear me and to come quickly to realign my thinking.

I have also been very aware that we have a hard time hearing God speak when we are preoccupied with worry, stress, or unbelief. God wants to talk to us. He wants to direct our lives and give us good gifts.

My life dramatically changed after this encounter with God. The major change that took place was that I stopped crying over everything that went wrong and talking about my problems over and over again. I had a newfound trust in God's plan for my life.

Some of the other changes that took place were we were introduced to tithing, which I will talk about in another section. Also, I was beginning to see the benefit of true worship, listening to the voice of God, and obeying the word of the Lord.

During this time, the Lord started to give me wisdom that I could speak to my husband to change his thinking concerning his employment. With these two changes in our thinking and obedience, our financial situation started to change.

Isaiah 45:19 tells us,

I publicly proclaim bold promises. I do not whisper obscurities in some dark corner. I would not have told the people of Israel to seek me if I could not be found. I, the LORD, speak only what is true and declare only what is right.

Isaiah 45:19 (NLT)

Faith comes from hearing and hearing the Word of God. Romans, chapter 10, states so clearly in the Amplified Bible what faith looks like and where faith comes from.

Our Righteousness Comes from God

These next verses are taken from the Everyday Life Bible by Joyce Meyers. Romans 10:3 says, **"For not knowing about God's righteousness [which is based on faith], and seeking to establish their own [righteousness based on works], they did not submit to God's righteousness."** Verse 4 says, **"For Christ is the end of the law [it leads to Him, and its purpose is fulfilled in Him], for [granting] righteousness to everyone who believes [in Him as Savior]"** (Romans 10:4, AMP).

Did you get what these verses are saying? We do not need to establish our own righteousness (right standing before God). We have the privilege of believing that Jesus fulfilled the law, that we can now trust in Him who satisfied the justice that God demanded for our sinfulness. Verses 8 to 11 speak to us of how we receive God's righteousness.

> **But what does it say?** "**The Word is near to you, in your mouth and in your heart**"—that is, the word [the message, the basis] of faith which we preach—because if you acknowledge and confess with your mouth that Jesus is Lord [recognizing His power, authority, and majesty as God] and believe in your heart that God raised Him from the dead, you will be saved. For with the heart a person believes [in Christ as Savior] resulting in his justification [that is, being made righteous—being freed from the guilt of sin and made acceptable to God]; and with the mouth he acknowledges and confesses [his faith openly], resulting in and confirming [his] salvation. For the scripture says, "**Whoever believes in Him** [whoever adheres to, trusts in, and relies on

Him] **WILL NOT BE DISAPPOINTED** [in his expectations]."

Romans 10:8–11 (AMP)

The Invitation to Know God Is Open to Everyone Who Believes!

Verses 12 and 13 speak of the invitation to everyone.

For there is no distinction between Jew and Gentile; for the same Lord is Lord over all [of us], and [He is] abounding in riches (blessings) for all who call on Him [in faith and prayer]. For "WHOEVER CALLS ON THE NAME OF THE LORD [in prayer] WILL BE SAVED."

Romans 10:12–13 (AMP)

Let us understand what this meant for the Jewish people at the time of these writings. The Jewish people understood that their "right standing" with God was based on the Mosaic Law, the Ten Commandments that Moses brought from God to the people along with the ones that were added on as the years went by. The Law stated if they obeyed, then they would be blessed, but if they disobeyed, they would be cursed. Part of God's mercy was a sacrificial system. The animal would bear the punishment in place of the person or family. This sacrifice would cover the sins of the people for a season.

The Jewish people also believed that males needed to be circumcised to be under the covenant that God had made with Abraham. This covenant was made before the Law. It was a covenant of faith and blessings to those who honored Abraham, which in turn meant they were honoring Yahweh, who Abraham had put his trust in. Abraham had left his family, who were not worshipping the One true God, to learn to follow and trust Him.

The Jewish people looked at anyone who was not under these covenants to be unclean or defiled (kind of how some Christians look at nonbelievers today). But here we find Paul telling everyone that Jesus has come and satisfied God and is now opening up a new way to have relationship with Him. There is no longer Jew and Gentile. There is not a set of rules or regulations to follow, but it is a change of heart and mind that leads you to want to obey out of love and respect for what Jesus has done.

It is kind of awesome if you think about it: God the Father accepts Jesus' sacrifice, so we are blessed. And we accept Jesus' sacrifice, so we are blessed, and, in the middle, we all become one family.

But How Do You Find Truth?

So, the question is, how do people find this truth? Isn't it great that the Spirit of truth revealed to Paul and now to us how we receive this revelation of God's righteousness?

> **But how will people call on Him in whom they have not believed? And how will they believe in Him of whom they have not heard? And how will they hear without a preacher**

(messenger)? And how will they preach unless they are commissioned and sent [for that purpose]? Just as it is written and forever remains written, "How beautiful are the feet of those who bring good news of good things!" But they did not all pay attention to the *good news* [of salvation]; for Isaiah says, "Lord, who has believed our report?" So faith comes from hearing [what is told], and what is heard comes by the [preaching of the] message concerning Christ.

Romans 10:14–17 (AMP)

(Hereinafter, emphasis added.)

We have to stop and ask: What is being told? What is being preached? And who is it that has not believed? Jesus went to His own, and His own did not receive Him. Does that mean that the people did not receive Him or His truth? No, that cannot be; otherwise, we would not have the New Testament and the writers of the Gospel. Christianity started with the Jewish people.

But did those who were in charge of preaching to the people believe Jesus? Sadly, many of them did not, and they were the ones that God used to send His Son, with permission from Jesus, to the cross. Jesus did it willingly, but the hardened hearts were where the providential hand of God came in to fulfill the plan of God in the natural realm.

Are You a Preacher Sent from God?

The question that must be asked now is, are you a preacher sent from God? Do you have a life-changing, Spirit-filled believing message of Good News for those you are sent to minister to?

If you are a preacher of the Word, a messenger sent from God to deliver the Good News to a lost world, please make sure you are telling the correct message! "For it is by grace you have been saved, through faith and it is not from yourselves, it is the gift of God, not by works so that no one can boast" (Ephesians 2:8–9, NIV).

Because, as I have seen in my own life, a little twisting of the Word, a little omission of the truth, a little misinformation of the Gospel (before or after salvation) can lead to a disastrous life of pain and shame.

CHAPTER 5

What Can You Do With an Apple?

The third dream of significance was somewhat different and took much longer to realize and come into existence.

This dream was about apples. In my dream, I saw apples, lots of apples. There were Red and Golden Delicious apples, Granny Smith and Macintosh, Fuji and Gala, Honeycrisp and Cortland. There were some on the trees and some in baskets.

As I walked around the apples, I heard myself ask, "What is so big about these apples?" At first, the answer to my question did not help me to understand the significance of them. The answer was more like a riddle to me: "What can you do with an apple?" So, in my dream, I paused and thought about it and then replied, "You can eat them; you can cook with them (pies, apple sauce, cake fillings); you can slice them and put them on pork chops; you can dry them out for chips or potpourri; you can crush them to make apple juice or cider, you can ferment the apples with sugar and water to make vinegar, and you can dry them out to make Halloween decorations. (They turn into scary faces.)

"Apples are very versatile and can be used in many ways. What else do you know about apples?" I was asked. My response was, "Some are sweet, some are tart, some are hard and remain that way, while others soften up when cooked. They have different colors and slightly different shapes. But they are all nutritious, good for our digestion, and may even help fight bad breath."

Did you know that there are over 7500 varieties grown throughout the world? Two thousand five hundred varieties are grown in the US, and one hundred of those varieties are commercially grown in the US.

After my dream, I thought I had never really thought that much about apples or their uses, but what does all this mean? Here again, is the simplest explanation that took years to be revealed. "You will be like the apple."

That was it! "You will be like the apple!"

Apples Take Time to Grow!

Do you know that once an apple tree is planted and its root system has been established, it takes about three years to produce its first fruits? After getting married, I took my freedom for granted and continued to make poor choices. But I can say that once I yielded my life to Jesus, for real this time, I then spent three years fasting and praying and studying God's Word before I started seeing any fruit being produced in my life.

Also, do you know that most apple tree varieties are not self-pollinating, but there need to be two different varieties close to each other so they and their flowers can be pollinated by bees? Without cross-pollination, the fruit will not grow from the flower. (The flower comes before the fruit.) I learned all of this when we purchased some apple trees and needed to know where and how to plant them. The man at the nursery was extremely helpful.

I cannot help but think of Jesus when He talks about us being in Him and that apart from Him, we can do nothing. **John 15:5 (NLT)** states, "Yes, I am the vine; you are the branches. Those who remain in me, and I in them, will produce much fruit. For apart from me you can do nothing."

Not only do we need to be attached to the branch to grow, but we also need to stay close to each other and give and take from each other to grow properly. Just like a certain variety of trees can self-pollinate, we can learn by ourselves. But just as it might be hard for us to learn from each other, when we do, we will be stronger and better, just as cross-pollinating will produce stronger plants.

Usefulness in God's Eye

So, what does all this have to do with being like an apple? Simply put, over the years, God has used me in many ways, in many different ministries, and with many different peoples. I have been asked or volunteered at our church over the years to be a Sunday school teacher, lead a mission trip, head up the recreation team and craft team for VBS, be a small group Bible study leader, be on the greeting team and the usher team, create women's events, and work hand in hand with some of the women pastors.

In my personal life, I have mentored and housed girls who have been incarcerated. I have worked with, housed, and mentored children who have been hospitalized for mental illness and trauma. I have worked with school systems as an advocate for students, as well as working in the lunchroom and in the school as the librarian. I have worked with and alongside doctors, counselors, psychiatrists, therapists, and social workers.

I have opened and run my own Christian day care with children whose parents are highly educated and parents who could barely afford to pay for my services. During that time, my daughter and I took a class on how to self-publish a book, and we wrote and published a children's ABC book for preschoolers. I have also owned and created a home bakery.

In my community, I have been a Girl Scout leader, a council member, a team mother to the cheerleader squads, created and wrote the weekly newsletter for the gymnastic team on which my daughter participated. I also organized and ran our neighborhood block parties. I have helped at food pantries and neighborhood service projects. I have been a caterer and an event planner. I have had weddings at my home and all kinds of social engagements.

So, at sixty-one years old, I can look back at all the ways God has used my life and all the people He has had me develop relationships with so that His fruits could be shared with those He loves and cares for.

I have been a student, a teacher, a mentor, and a friend, but the one thing that has never changed is that I have studied the Bible day in and day out, in season and out of season. In doing so, I have found the Lord has been faithful to continually teach me, develop me, steer me in the right direction, strengthen me, and bless me.

My prayer is that I have been a sweet aroma and that as people have interacted with me, they are able to "taste and see that the LORD is good; blessed is the one who takes refuge in Him" (Psalm 34:8, NIV).

God has indeed used me in a variety of ways and in a variety of settings. It is interesting to me that the Lord always let me know ahead of time just what I would be doing prior to my doing it, and I would be waiting with expectancy for the opportunity to present itself to enter into God's will in that area.

God Wires Us for His Purposes

What is hard about this life is that, at times, it seems so unsettling to me. I look around and see people who have years of schooling or years of being in the same job or profession, and they seem so settled, and yet, I have to constantly ask God to lead me in the way that I should go and then listen with an open heart and ear. (But doesn't every Christian have to live this way?)

But God, in His wisdom, knew that. That is how He wired me. I get bored easily. I love to create things, solve problems, and find the simplest way to accomplish something. I like to instruct people, and I love to study the Word of God.

Through all of these experiences, I have learned that truth takes time to understand and work its way from our heads to our hearts and then out into the world through our lives. And often, we do not understand or apply it to our lives the first time that we encounter it.

The truth is that anyone who follows Jesus has to go through the same steps, even if it appears different on the outside. We all need to be constantly asking what His will for us is in any and all situations!

Growing Up Is Not Always Easy

As I look at the growth process in my life, I realize that not all these experiences were pleasant for me, and I had to allow the Lord to use me as He felt fit to do. There were times that I felt like I was being squeezed and pressed down like an apple would be to make cider. Second Corinthians 4:8–10 reads,

We are hard pressed on every side, but not crushed; perplexed, but not in despair; persecuted, but not abandoned; struck down, but not destroyed. We always carry around in our body the death of Jesus, so that

the life of Jesus may also be revealed in our body.

2 Corinthians 4:8–10 (NIV)

There were times I thought it was a sweet situation that I was walking into, but I soon found out I was over my head and in the dark and could not get my head above the water. It was like apples being put in a jar of water sprinkled with sugar being weighed down, placed in the dark until the fullness of the fermentation is complete and the vinegar is ready for use.

There were also times when I heard God's voice but was too afraid to respond. This caused me a lot of pain. One such instance was when I was to leave my position as a specialized foster parent. I loved that job, but situations were arising, and the Lord told me to leave; but I had done it for so long it was as though I did not know who I would be if not "the specialized foster mom."

I became anxious, and the anxiety caused stress, induced asthma, which gave me shortness of breath and woke me up at night not being able to breathe. Finally, I heard the Lord say, "If you don't quit, you will die." It is sad but necessary that in those times, you realize in what or whom you really trust. I was trusting in my job; I also found acceptance in my reputation and people needing my help and advice.

I am not saying we should not help or mentor people in need. But when we make our life all about the person, place, or thing, and we lose our first love (Jesus), we distort what and why God has called us to do His work. Along the way, we lose something incredibly special, His tender voice directing us, assuring us, and correcting or redirecting us as we go.

Again, we can do nothing apart from Him. Sometimes we think we are doing His will, but if we are anxious constantly and cannot hear Him clearly, then our relationship with Him is out of whack, and we need to stop and ask for directions.

Thankfully, we serve a Father who loves us, a Friend who died for us, and a Spirit who never leaves us nor forsakes us. God knows how to get us back on track and give us new mercy every morning. I left that position and spent the next year being healed while working with young children at our church as a Mom-to-Mom lead teacher in the preschool room. At that time, God gave me a vision to open my own Christian day care with my daughter, which we did successfully for almost ten years. God is faithful!

CHAPTER 6

Where Does the Apple Come From?

I believe that God wants us to bear good fruit so that others will see a reflection of Jesus in our lives. I would like to walk through the steps that I feel I went through while maturity was taking place, so good fruit has or will be fully developed.

The apple is only as good as the tree it comes from, and the tree must go through different stages before it can produce fruit. We also must go through these stages of our spiritual life before we can bear good fruit. Let us look at what is needed for an apple tree to grow and produce fruit and then look at some correlations in our spiritual life:

As I studied the creation story in Genesis, chapters 1 and 2, I saw several parallels between our apple tree growth and our spiritual growth. Isn't it awesome how God uses nature to help us understand spiritual truths? In the next couple of chapters, I would like to examine light and darkness, the good soil and the Sower, Living Water, the underground activity taking place, a good rootstock, grafting, new seasons, nutrients, pruning, and drops.

But we cannot start to grow until we understand that there is a heavenly realm and an earthly realm. We, in our natural state, have been separated from the heavenly realm due to sin in the world and in our lives. Thankfully by the wisdom of God, Jesus came and brought the light into our world, allowing our faith by His grace to bring us back into union with God. That is where and when we begin to grow, and in doing so, we are seated in the heavenly realm with God.

So, let us get started!

Light, Darkness, and Water

When we think of fruit growing on a tree, we might not consider the importance of darkness. But God knew the role light and darkness would play in the growth and maturity of us and of trees. Genesis 1:1–2 tells us what the world was like prior to God speaking light into existence. It states,

In the beginning God created the heavens and the earth. Now the earth was formless and empty, darkness was over the surface of the deep, and the Spirit of God was hovering over the waters.

Genesis 1:1–2 (NIV)

Our world was formless and void, and darkness was over the face of the deep. But notice that the Spirit was hovering over the face of the waters.

Most seeds germinate best in darkness. Seeds do not necessarily need direct light but do need water, oxygen, and warm temperatures. Let us look to see what comes first.

Do you realize that there was darkness, water, and the Spirit of God before there was light?

In the beginning God created the heaven and the earth. And the earth was without *form*, and *void*; and *darkness* was upon the face of

> the deep. And the Spirit of God moved upon
> the face of the waters.

> Genesis 1:1–2 (KJV)

Have you ever thought about the fact that God created darkness?

> I am the LORD, and there is none else, there
> is no God beside me: I girded thee, though
> thou hast not known me:
> That they may know from the rising of the
> sun, and from the west, that there is none
> beside me. I am the LORD, and there is no
> one else.
> I form the light, and create darkness: I make
> peace, and create evil: I the LORD do all
> these things. [...] I the LORD have created it.
> [...] I have made the earth, and created man
> upon it:

> Isaiah 45:5–7, 8c, 12a (KJV)

These verses are referring to Cyrus, a pagan king whom God used mightily for His people. God was letting Cyrus know that He was the one and only God and that He (God) had called him (Cyrus) by name to deliver the children of Israel from oppression and to rebuild the temple. This was prophesied and recorded by Isaiah 200 years before Cyrus was born.

Prior to this revelation (light, knowledge), Cyrus believed that there was a god for good and a god for evil; he was in darkness. But once the knowledge and understanding came to Cyrus about Yahweh, the God of Israel, the one true God, he was able to accomplish what God had planned for him to do before he was even born, before he knew the one true God!

Stop and think for a moment. Is there anyone that you know who has not experienced darkness, void, or been without form? What do I mean, you may ask? Let us look at the words and their meanings.

"*Without form*," according to Strong's Concordance, comes from the Hebrew "tohuw," which can be to lie waste, worthless, confusion, an empty place, vanity, desolation (of surface), nothing, vain, or wilderness.

"*Void*," according to Strong's Concordance, comes from the Hebrew word "bohuw," which is to be empty, superficially, an undistinguishable ruin, or vacuity (lack of thought or intelligence, empty-headedness).

"*Darkness*," according to Strong's Concordance, comes from the Hebrew word "choshek" to mean misery, destruction, death, ignorance, sorrow, wickedness, and obscurity.

We all start out with one of these traits. There is not one person who starts out knowing God and doing everything perfectly. But God did not stop and leave us in darkness; no, the Holy Spirit moved upon the face of the waters. "And God said, 'Let there be light,' and there was light" (Genesis 1:3, NIV).

This is so exciting to me because I am so aware that the Holy Spirit is the One who knows the deep things of God. First Corinthians 2:9–10 speaks of this...

But as it is written:

"Eye has not seen, nor ear heard,

Nor have entered into the heart of man

The things which God has prepared for those

who love Him."

But God has revealed them to us through His

Spirit. For the Spirit searches all things, yes,

the deep things of God.

1 Corinthians 2:9–10 (NKJV)

If the Holy Spirit were not moving among people and hovering over me, seeing my lost condition, my useless life, and my heart that was void of the truth of God's love for me, and if God did not have the wisdom to know that we needed the Light to illuminate our hearts and the Holy Spirit to reveal the wisdom of God to us, I would never have been found. I would not even know to go looking for Him; I would have been dead in sin and meaningless searching to fill the void in my heart.

Just like in the beginning, God knew when to send the light into the darkness, so He knows when to let the light shine in our lives so we can begin to grow.

The Importance of Light

Have you ever thought about the importance of light and what it does for us? Light illuminates, it brings warmth, it causes things to grow, it helps us to see in the darkness so we do not lose our way, it helps us find things that are lost.

Let us look at what Genesis tells us about the light that God spoke into existence. "Then God said, 'Let there be light'; and there was light. And God saw the light that it was good; and God divided the light from the darkness" (Genesis1:3–4, NKJV).

Did you catch what that last phrase said? God divided light from darkness. He separated them; He distinguished one from the other. Just like in nature, there needs to be light, so do our hearts need the light of truth. When Jesus, the Word of truth, enters our lives, He does the work of separating us from the darkness. We become aware of the spiritual world; we sense the warmth of God's love; we learn to live in and acknowledge truth that brings wholeness to our lives.

Also, when we look at nature, we see that "The Word" was spoken, and light came into the natural world. When we look at the spiritual world, we see that "The Written Word" also speaks light into us. Without "The Written Word," we would have no understanding of God's love for us, His majesty, His glory, and the gospel of His Son. Second Corinthians 4:4 (KJV) reads, "In whom the god of this world hath blinded the minds of them which believe not, lest the light of the glorious gospel of Christ, who is the image of God, should shine unto them."

When we consider our natural world and our spiritual world, we see that God, the Holy Spirit, and the Word (Jesus) were at the beginning together creating life. We also see that through the power of the Holy Spirit and by the direction of God the Father, Jesus was conceived of a virgin to be born into our natural world so we might have spiritual life.

John 1:1–5 says,

In the beginning was the Word: The Word was with God and the Word was God. He was with God in the beginning. Through him all things came to be, not one thing had its being but through Him. All that came to be had life in Him and that life was the light of men, and that light shines in the dark, a light that darkness could not overpower.

John 1:1–5 (TJB)

These verses are also showing us that we need Jesus' life in order to have the light that we need to grow. When we start to see Jesus and experience His love, His life is what brings light that shines in our dark hearts. The more we hear about Jesus and can accept it as truth, the more the darkness is removed, and the more understanding we have about the Father and how much He loves us. The Holy Spirit knows where those dark places are in our lives, or better said, in our hearts. He knows what we need to hear and when it is the best time for us to hear a certain truth about Jesus. The Spirit of God is able to penetrate our dark hard heart and soften it as we hear about God sending Jesus to pay for our penalty of sin and restoring us to a relationship with Him.

Jesus, Himself, tells us that He is the light of the world. When Jesus spoke to the people again, He said, "I am the light of the world; anyone who follows Me will not be walking in the dark; he will have the light of life" (**John 8:12, NLV**). Let us make sure we catch some important words, "anyone who follows Me, will not be walking in darkness." Jesus will lead, and it is our responsibility to follow Him.

Paul confirms this truth in **2 Corinthians 4:6 (NIV)**, "For God, who said, 'Let light shine out of darkness,' made his light shine in our hearts to give us the light of the knowledge of God's glory displayed in the face of Christ."

So, in nature, we see that before there were trees for fruit to grow on, there was darkness and light. As we have stated earlier, we all have been in spiritual darkness and need the light of "The Word" to shine in our hearts. We all need to have some understanding of Jesus and what He has done for us, how much we need Him, that He is God and has come from God and is in perfect union with God, and that He died for our sins, was buried, and rose again. We need the light of the Gospel revealed to us before we begin to grow.

Jesus Separates Us

Also, we need to know that Jesus came to separate us from our chaos, wickedness, and blindness. I was thinking of the word "separation." Do you realize that God separated Adam and Eve from the Garden of Eden so they would not eat of the tree of life and be stuck in their guilt and condemnation?

Noah was separated from the sinful people of his times when he entered the ark. He had been preaching to them the entire time that he was building the ark, and yet they did not believe his words. They mocked him and laughed at him because they had never seen a flood.

Abraham was told to separate himself from his family, that were idol worshippers: in doing so, he was able to see and hear the promises God had for his family and the families of the earth.

Joseph was separated from his father so he could save a nation as well as his family.

Moses was separated from his people so he would learn how to lead them and so they could survive in a place with which they were unfamiliar.

Joshua and Caleb were separated from the other ten spies, and because they had a different spirit, they were able to lead and win victories with the people in the Promised Land.

And finally, Jesus called out the twelve disciples to change the world.

When we trust enough to be obedient to God's call for us to come out of the darkness and come to the True Light, Jesus, it is so He can show His grace, mercy, and love, and in doing so, He blesses us and blesses others through us.

Do you also see that God spoke to each of those people, gave them revelation of a promise, and they believed Him, but each one had to grow into maturity before he saw the fruit of his faith come into reality?

Let the Soil Sprout Life

God also separated the waters first to make the heavens, and then He separated them so that there would be seas and earth.

Then God said, "Let the waters below the heavens be gathered into one place [of standing, pooling together] and let the dry

land appear"; and it was so. God called the dry land earth, and the gathering of the waters He called seas; and God saw that this was good (pleasing, useful) and He affirmed and sustained it. So, God said, "Let the earth sprout [tender] vegetation, plants yielding seed, and fruit trees bearing fruit according to (limited to, consistent with) their kind, whose seed is in them upon the earth"; and it was so.

Genesis 1:9–11 (AMP)

When we look at what God did and said, we see that it was good to separate the dry land and the waters. And then He said, "Let the earth sprout vegetation, plants yielding seed and fruit bearing trees." All of the plants, fruits, and vegetables came out of the good soil. Notice there were no painful toiling in tending the garden before sin entered the earth. Also, the ground had not produced thorns or thistles.

But what happened when Adam sinned? The curse came in, and the soil now had thorns and thistles growing out of it (we will explore the thorns and thistles in a later segment of this chapter). When we look at our analogy, we see that our soil (our heart) has also been affected by the curse, so instead of good soil, we have soil or a heart that produces evil.

The curse had literal effects on Adam and Eve. They were told to leave the garden and the abundance of good and health-giving fruit that was in it, and instead, they would eat the plants of the field. Adam was also told that through painful sorrow, he would toil the ground and eat food from it all the days of his life. And lastly, the scripture tells us that by the sweat of Adam's brow, he would eat his food until he died and returned to the ground from which he came.

And because of the curse, we have been spiritually separated from God, from His abundance of life-giving food, and we now toil and labor knowing that there are both good and harmful thoughts and intentions in our hearts.

So how did God deal with this sin in our hearts? The answer is simple...Jesus!

Galatians 3:13 (KJV) states, **"Christ hath redeemed us from the curse of the law, being made a curse for us: for it is written, cursed is every one that hangeth on a tree."**

Second Corinthians 5:17 tells us that if we are in Christ, we are a new creation. **"Therefore, if anyone is in Christ, he is a new creation; old things have passed away; behold, all things have become new"** (2 Corinthians 5:17, NKJV).

How does this happen to us? Ezekiel 36:26 (KJV) tells us, **"A new heart also will I give you, and a new spirit will I put within you: and I will take away the stony heart out of your flesh, and I will give you a heart of flesh."**

Because Jesus has redeemed us from the curse of the law, we, by the power of God, can receive a new heart that will allow the word of truth to grow from our new hearts (the good soil).

In the Genesis 1:9–11 passage, there is a vital truth; God said that what He had made was good, and He affirmed and sustained it. When God's Seed (Jesus) enters our hearts, God sees it as good. We must never forget that God affirms and sustains what He has called into being.

What I have discovered is that light is vital to every seed after germination because, without sunlight, the little sprout will not survive if it cannot reach a light source. Once the seed (the Word of God) starts to open up in our hearts, we must keep our eyes on Jesus. We must look upward until we are fully immersed with the light of truth.

Germination

So now, let us explore the significance of the soil. I was going to start with the root system, but then I thought, there is a seed before there is a root. Have you ever thought about how a plant or tree begins? It starts with a sower dropping a seed into soil, and the seed needs water. Germination is the process of the seed developing into a new plant or tree. We put the seed into the ground or soil, and then we water it.

When we plant grass, we put it on the soil, scratch it in, and then we water it. The seed needs water to grow. When water is plentiful, the seed fills with water in a process called imbibition. The water then activates special proteins called enzymes, which begin the process of seed growth. But then we wait!

Mark 4:26–29 explains this truth,

And He said, "The kingdom of God is as if a man should scatter seed on the ground, and should sleep by night and rise by day, and the seed should sprout and grow, he himself does not know how. For the earth yields crops

by itself: first the blade, then the head, and

after that full grain in the head. But when

the grain ripens, immediately he puts in the

sickle, because the harvest has come."

Mark 4:26–29 (NKJV)

So we see that growth is taking place naturally, but we do not know how long it will take to mature.

What Grows Out of the Soil?

We have already looked at how the water was separated from the dry land. Now let us look at what came from the soil. Do you realize what came from the soil in our natural world?

Read Genesis, chapters 1 and 2, to see how God spoke the world into existence. We already read Genesis 1:11; let's also look at verse 12,

So God said, "Let the earth sprout [tender]

vegetation, plants yielding seeds, and fruit

trees bearing fruit according to (limited to,

consistent with) their kind, whose seed is in

them upon the earth"; and it was so.

The earth sprouted and abundantly produced

vegetation, plants yielding seed according to their kind, and trees bearing fruit with seed in them, according to their kind; and God saw that it was good and He affirmed and sustained it.

Genesis 1:11–12 (AMP)

We were also formed from the dust of the earth; Genesis 2:7 (TJB) reads as follows, "Yahweh God fashioned man of dust from the soil. Then he breathed into his nostrils a breath of life, and thus man became a living being." When the seed is planted in the good soil (the heart that is ready to produce) and the water has opened it, the soil starts to produce whatever is in that seed.

Genesis 2:9 tells us,

Yahweh God caused to spring up from the soil every kind of tree, enticing to look at and good to eat, with the tree of life and the tree of the knowledge of good and evil in the middle of the garden.

Genesis 2:9 (TJB)

"Yahweh God took the man and settled him in the garden of Eden to cultivate and take care of it" (Genesis 2:15, TJB). Genesis 2:19 also tells us that from the soil, Yahweh God fashioned all the wild beasts.

God uses nature to show us spiritual truths. For example, man is not only a natural being but a spiritual one. God breathed His life into Adam's nostrils; it was the breath of life to be human, but we are told in Genesis 1:27 that we are made in the image of God, which means we are moral beings, spiritual beings, and have an intellectual nature.

Then God said, "Let Us (Father, Son, Holy Spirit) make man in Our image, according to Our likeness [not physical, but a spiritual personality and moral likeness]; and let them have complete authority over the fish of the sea, the birds of the air, the cattle, and over the entire earth, and over everything that creeps and crawls on the earth." So God created man in His own image, in the image and likeness of God He created him; male and female He created them.

Genesis 1:26–27 (AMP)

But when sin entered the world, the spiritual life was cut off from God. God had said that in the day that Adam ate the fruit of the tree of the knowledge of good and evil, he would surely die. In that day, Adam became aware of his sin, and he hid from God; he tried to cover his sin and shame.

So let us review, God used the Word to bring life into existence and He uses the Word to bring life into our spiritual existence. The breath of God is His Spirit; without the Holy Spirit living in us, we are spiritually dead. The seed of God is the "Word" of God, Jesus.

God made plants for nourishment. He uses spiritual water that cleanses us and breaks open those hard places in our lives so that the good soil can produce life. Jesus is the Living Water for our souls and the Bread of Life from where we get our nourishment.

Adam was instructed to cultivate or tend to the garden; we are to do the same with our new hearts, which is our spiritual garden. We cultivate our hearts by drinking in truth and feeding on Jesus. Letting Him cleanse us with His Word, believing that we are His and that He Has lavished or, better yet, poured out His love on us.

God made the physical animals, one of which was sacrificed to cover Adam and Eve's nakedness, which came as a result of sin. God fashioned a body for Jesus, who is the Lamb of God that was sacrificed for the sin of the whole world.

God has placed before us the knowledge of good and evil, and He has invited us to partake of His grace that reminds us that God remembers our sin no more and that He is faithful to forgive our sins and to cleanse us from all unrighteousness. By grace through faith, we are invited into eternal spiritual life.

Chapter 7

Where Does Our Spiritual Fruit Come From?

So, how does growth start in our spiritual life? The Sower sows a seed; that is, He drops it into the soil. God is the Sower. The seed is the Word of God, and when it enters a receptive heart (the good soil), it will reproduce the life of God in us. But how does that seed get dropped into our life? Do we, as humans, seek God by our own nature? The answer is no. Romans 3:10–11 (NIV) states, "As it is written: 'There is no one righteous, not even one; there is no one who understands, there is no one that seeks God.'"

In nature, once sin entered the world, it caused the soil to be cursed, causing thorns and thistles to grow.

To Adam he said, "Because you listened

to your wife and ate the fruit from the tree

about which I commanded you, 'You must

not eat from it,'

"Cursed is the ground because of you;

through painful toil you will eat food from it

all the days of your life.

It will produce thorns and thistles for you,

and you will eat the plants of the field."

Genesis 3:17–18 (NIV)

Because of sin's effect on the earth, man now needed to till the soil. But just as the ground on the earth was not able to produce only the good fruit, our hearts are filled with the sin nature and are incapable of producing good fruit on their own.

Now that sin has entered into our hearts, there is rebellion, self-interest, disobedience, and every evil thought. We need the soil of our lives to be tilled so that thorns and thistles can stop dominating our lives. Without the work of the Holy Spirit, no one has the right heart attitude to seek God. "For I know that good itself does not dwell in me, that is, in my sinful nature. For I have the desire to do what is good, but I cannot carry it out" (Romans 7:18, NIV).

Psalm 14:2–3 tells us,

The LORD looks down from heaven on all mankind

to see if there are any who understand,

any who seek God.

All have turned away; all have become corrupt;

there is no one that does good,

not even one.

Psalm 14:2–3 (NIV)

It is the Spirit of God that is doing the work to prepare our hearts. The only way we are saved is when the Spirit draws us to

Jesus. John 6:44 (NIV) makes this noticeably clear, "No man can come to me, except the Father which hath sent me, draw him; and I will raise him up, at the last day." Ephesians 2:8 (NIV) tells us how we are able to receive this new life that God wants to grow in us: "For it is by grace you have been saved, through faith—and this is not from yourselves; it is the gift of God."

A lot of people have the misunderstanding that they have found God, but it is quite the opposite. Jesus is the Good Shepherd who goes out and finds us. Think about this; the soil does not go to the seed, but the seed goes to the soil. The Sower has to make room for the seed. There are different ways of planting a seed depending on its needs. The Sower might dig a hole by pushing the dirt to the side, creating a space for the plant and roots to fit comfortably in.

Or He may simply push the seed down into the soft earth or scrape and soften the surface and lay the seed on the softened soil, hoping the wind and the birds do not remove it from the location where He wants growth.

He may also have to remove rocks that would get in the way of the growth of the tree or remove weeds that would choke out the baby sapling.

No matter the depth, the Sower has to move or remove some of the soil to let the new seed have a place to grow. The Good Sower also makes sure the nutrients are sufficient for the plant's growth in the soil and that the weeds are removed. We have also looked at how without water, the seed will not germinate. We need the Living Water to be poured over us.

Because we are incapable of knowing the things of God apart from the Helper, we need the Holy Spirit and the Word of God to be brought to us in order for our spiritual growth to begin. Romans 3:10–12 shows us how much our old way of thinking has to be removed or replaced with the truth of God's salvation, His will, and His ways. It states,

> **"There is none righteous, no, not one;**
>
> **There is none that understands,**
>
> **There is none that seeks after God.**
>
> **They have all turned aside;**
>
> **They have together become unprofitable;**
>
> **There is none who does good,   no, not one."**
>
> **Romans 3:10–12 (NKJV)**

But God, by His grace, sent His message of salvation to man by Jesus and through the power of the Holy Spirit and through the preaching of the Gospel. "The Spirit gives life, the flesh counts for nothing. The words I have spoken to you—they are full of the Spirit and life" (John 6:63, NIV).

> **Nevertheless I tell you the truth. It is to your**
>
> **advantage that I go away; for if I do not go**
>
> **away, the Helper will not come to you; but if**
>
> **I depart, I will send Him to you. And when**
>
> **He has come, He will convict the world of**
>
> **sin, and of righteousness, and of judgment:**

of sin, because they do not believe in Me; of righteousness, because I go to my Father and you see Me no more; of judgment, because the ruler of this world is judged.

John 16:7–11 (NKJV)

Romans 10:13 (NIV) tells us, "Everyone who calls on the name of the Lord will be saved." But how can they call on Him to save them unless they believe in Him? And how can they believe in Him if they have never heard about Him? And how can they hear about Him unless someone tells them? And how will anyone go and tell them without being sent? That is why the Scripture says, "How beautiful are the feet of messengers who bring good news!" (Romans 10:15b, NIV)

Not everyone, of course, listens to the Good News. As Isaiah says: "Lord how many believed what we proclaimed?" (Romans 10:16, TJB)

Once we have believed the message of our salvation through Jesus' death, burial, and resurrection, we are told to seek the Lord continually. "Seek the LORD and his strength, seek his face continually" (1 Chronicles 16:11, KJV). And Jeremiah assures us that if we do seek Him with our whole heart, we will find Him. Jeremiah 29:13 (NKJV) states, "And you will seek Me and find Me, when you search for Me with all your heart."

When I was a young child, I heard many stories about Jesus and how much He loved me. My favorite song was, "Jesus loves me, this I know, for the Bible tells me so./Little ones to Him belong; they are weak, but He is strong." And "The B_I_B_L_E, yes that's the book for me,/I stand alone on the Word of God, the B_I_B_L_E."

So, faith comes from what is preached, and what is preached comes from the Word of God, and the Holy Spirit reveals these truths to our spirit, so we can have them start to grow in our hearts.

God, Himself, spoke to human beings, and they wrote His words for us to know Him. Not only did He give us His written word, but John tells us in His gospel that "the Word became flesh and dwelt among us" (John 1:14, NKJV). The Word, Jesus, came not only to save us from our sins but to let us know Who God is and how much He desires us to have a relationship with Himself.

I had faith growing in me because, as a child, I was told of Jesus' love and death and payment for my sins. And I understood that I wanted to be friends with Jesus, and I wanted to have a relationship with Him. I asked Jesus into my heart at a summer day camp program. God saw that it was good; He affirmed that the Seed was planted in good soil (my heart), and He sustained it until the proper time for the process was to develop.

We Need Living Water

As we continue to read and study the Word of God, the Holy Spirit, which is the Living Water, is at work softening our hearts and enabling the love of God and the truth of His Son to start to grow in us. It becomes alive in us just as the seed opens and begins to grow roots. Ezekiel 36:25–27 tells us:

I shall pour clean water over you, and you
will be cleansed; I shall cleanse you of all
your defilement and all your idols. I shall give
you a new heart and put a new spirit in you;
I shall remove the heart of stone from your

**bodies and give you a heart of flesh instead.
I shall put my Spirit in you, and make you
keep my laws and sincerely respect my
observances.**

Ezekiel 36:25–27 (TJB)

Most of us do not realize that our hearts are hard and that we do not want to trust God's way to peace and fulfillment. We think we are rather good, kind, and generous and that all these things will please God and satisfy us. But without Jesus in our life, we know deep down inside us that something is missing, and we go looking for the "thing" to fill us and satisfy us. Jesus tells us that the only way we will be satisfied is to drink the Living Water that He provides.

Jesus tells us in John 4:13–14,

**Whoever drinks this water [natural water]
will get thirsty again; but anyone who drinks
the water [spiritual water, allowing the Spirit
to open those seeds of truth that have been
placed within you] that I shall give, will never
be thirsty again: the water that I shall give
will turn into a spring inside him, welling up
to eternal life.**

John 4:13–14 (TJB)

I learned the hard way that unless we get the truth of who Jesus is and what He has done for us, we will never be satisfied. I was searching for peace and safety, but because my search was looking in the wrong direction, I was not satisfied.

Do you have that spring welling up in you? Have you let the Spirit of God soften your heart and cause you to be obedient to the promptings He gives? Have you accepted the cleansing that only God can do through the death of Jesus and His blood sacrifice for us? Have you put God and His Word (Jesus is the Word, come in the flesh) first in your life? Or are you trying to satisfy your hurts or longings with some other means? These questions are particularly important because if you cannot answer them with a definite "Yes!" then you need to consider what you believe and why. Only a true relationship with Jesus will heal you and allow you to have a relationship with the Father.

Jesus, Himself, told us: "I am the way, the truth, and the life: no man cometh unto the Father, but by me" (John 14:6, KJV).

What's Happening Underground?

The next stage in the life of a plant or tree is that the seed grows a root to access water underground. This is the part of a plant that attaches it to the ground or to a support. In the apple tree, this would be underground, and it brings water and nourishment to the rest of the plant through multiple branches and fibers. I believe the root in our lives is the desire to know God and be fed by Him. Roots go searching for water and nutrients. When the water is scarce, it causes the root to go down deeper into the soil and search out what it needs to feed the tree. Roots also expand and spread out around the plant.

God is not only the Sower but the one who sends the water, and sometimes He holds back the rain from above, so we will search for it below. God's Word tells us to search for God as a hidden treasure, and when we seek Him with our whole hearts, we will find Him. This searching takes place as we study the Word, spend time in prayer, and cry out to God with our questions or concerns. The Spirit is already in us, and through the daily study of the Word, we find that Living Water that refreshes us.

There are seasons in our lives when we feel or think that we cannot see or hear God, so do not be discouraged. Remember, God has promised that He will never leave us or forsake us. But remember, God has a timing for all things. So instead of worrying or believing the lies that the enemy might be whispering in your ear, be faithful to what God has called you to do. Give your time and effort in studying His Word, and keep your mind open and your eyes fixed on Him. Think about His goodness, His faithfulness, and your past experiences with Him.

Sing praises to Him in this season, be obedient to His calling, honor Him with your words and actions because He inhabits the praises of His people. By this, I mean that you will sense His presence as you worship Him. Worship may come by praising Him during your difficulties, or it may be by your obedience to something you would rather not do, or it may be giving up something you have been holding on to. God loves when we trust Him in all circumstances. He never leaves us nor forsakes us. The beauty of God's working is that when that season is over, you will see how He was with you all along and guided your footsteps all the way and produced something in you that others will now see!

This season of searching and waiting on God is when your roots will grow deeper. You will learn more of God's faithfulness to you and see Him in an incredibly special way. But if your roots do not go searching for the water of God's Word, they will remain shallow, and when storms come, you will not have the depth and security to weather them.

I had a situation that really made me question God's love and protection. My roots were really shallow, and I did not know at the time to go deeper into the scriptures to find what God's Word promised. When I was in elementary school, we owned a station wagon. At the time, we would all pile in the back of the car without seatbelts and bring our friends with us. In our neighborhood, we played with thirty or so friends. We would bring them to church activities at different times.

One day I brought my friend to church. She had a disease named cystic fibrosis. It was incurable when we were growing up. It affects the cells that produce mucus, sweat, and digestive juices. It causes the fluids to become sticky and thick. They then plug up tubes, ducts, and passageways. My friend had to sleep in an oxygen tent every night and take numerous medications daily.

While we were at church, we were running around outside the building. Between the doors, there was a large glass window without any bars. She thought it was an open door and ran straight through it. She was rushed to the hospital. She stayed in the intensive care unit for over a month. When she returned home, she had over one hundred stitches going up her legs, inside and out. She had to remain inside for the next three months and had to take several more medications throughout the day for infections and to keep her blood flowing properly.

The result of that incident was that our families became enemies. Her dad hated our family. She and I were still friends, but we could not play together if her dad was home. I also do not remember bringing anyone else to church with us after that accident.

The most difficult result of this incident was, if I can say this right, is that it put a seed of doubt in my heart. And that seed grew as more and more difficult situations entered my life. No one taught me to dig into the Scriptures to find a loving God who could heal those hurts. By the time she was twenty-one, I had lost any sense of God in my life, as my friend died alone at an early age from her disease.

Also, notice that all of this pain was taking place underground, in the dark. No one else saw what I was going through. They may have seen the tears; they may have heard the frustration and may even have been aware of the outward circumstances that made me cry out. But they never really knew what I was longing for, what my true heart desire was, that question that only God in His wisdom and love could answer for me: where are You?

The Spirit Knows the Deep Things of God

But let us go back to the creation and see that the Holy Spirit knows the deep things of God. He saw my lost condition, my heart that was void of the truth. He knew how to take what the enemy meant for evil and, in His time and His ways, use it for good.

This wonderful truth that Jesus knows our every hurt and need, that He came to heal us and bring us into a place of peace, came to me a little later in my life; it came as a result of seeking to know God personally and as I started searching the Bible for myself. I found a loving God who has a good plan for my life and yet allows circumstances in my life to be used for His glory in His timing and according to His purposes. I also realized that my decisions had a lot to do with my circumstances, and they were not a result of God's doing.

So now, I do not spend so much time searching for "things" to satisfy my needs or running away from God when things are not going exactly as I thought they should. I now find myself going straight to the source, Jesus, and letting His Spirit fill me anew with His love, provisions, and perspective.

I have found that these painful times can also be private times between you and your loving Savior, and you should treasure them as such; because, in your weakness, as you are searching for Him, you will learn to depend on His strength. In your awareness of sin, you will learn to be dependent on His truth of grace and forgiveness. With your questions and waiting on Him, you will learn to be still and hear His voice.

Spiritual Growth Should be Instinctual

Spiritual growth becomes instinctual in our lives. It may not seem like it at the time we are growing but think of babies learning to walk. They need to be fed milk daily, and as they grow and develop, they need more substantial food, so their muscles will grow and develop. They do not feed themselves, and we do not give them junk food. But they do cry for food, and if we are good parents, we will give our babies the most nutritious milk and food to get them started in life.

I raised four of my own children, took in foster children, and had a day care for several years. I learned to watch how children grow and develop. I found that they are not aware that each time they roll over, they are learning to move their body. Each time they sit up with a pillow propping them up, they are developing posture and muscles, and soon they will learn from memory how to stay up. Each time they lift themselves from the ground and move those chubby little legs to crawl, they are becoming aware of their surroundings and that they can be independent. Each time they stand and hold onto a table or your hand to walk, they are learning courage and trust, and finally, each time they walk from one person to the next and fall, but get up again to continue, and you cheer them on, they are learning patience, tenacity, and that they are loved.

Soon they are running across the room and getting into everything. But they did all of it instinctually without our demanding anything from them. In fact, the more attention we give to them, the more they grow and desire to explore their new world. Our part may have been to prop them up and encourage them to crawl or walk to us. But unless they have the desire from within to do those things on their own, they will not get stronger. They will be limited in how they move about and experience life. We, as parents or caregivers, see their excitement and join in the learning process. We encourage them and give them boundaries, like gates and cabinet locks, to keep them safe.

As we grow spiritually, it should also be instinctual. In other words, we do not always know why we are doing something; we just feel we need to try to do it or ask God for what we need or feel the desire to explore His Word. This is true grace at work. It is the Holy Spirit who motivates us and encourages us to keep going. He is able also to redirect us so we will not get hurt. These things happen as we spend time in fellowship with Him and keep our eyes fixed on Jesus.

We also, as brothers and sisters in Christ, have the responsibility to encourage others if we have already gone through that developmental stage.

Finally, we must remember that there are many different stages to our spiritual growth as we continue to grow in the knowledge and likeness of Jesus each step of the way.

One blessing that became instinctual for my husband and me is tithing. I remember when Jesus first spoke to us about tithing. My husband and I had both lost our jobs in the fall of the previous year. We had a car payment, mortgage payment, and credit card bills. We were living on unemployment and credit.

One day while in church, the pastor spoke on tithing and read the scripture from Malachi 3:10 it reads,

"Bring the whole tithe into the storehouse,

that there may be food in my house. Test me

in this," says the LORD Almighty, "and see if I

will not throw open the floodgates of heaven

and pour out so much blessing that there will

not be room enough to store it."

Malachi 3:10 (NIV)

Up until this point, we had given freely to family members but had not really given on a consistent basis to our church. I felt the Lord tell me to trust Him and be obedient to give the amount He laid on my heart. To be fair, the amount was more than 10 percent. And it was more than we could afford at the time.

This was a new learning experience for us. There were weeks when we did not have enough money to pay both the tithe and our bills. But I soon learned that when I trusted God, I was always able to pay the bills somehow as well as pay the tithe.

While we were learning to trust with the tithe, we were also learning how to pay down our bills without any help from others. The Lord gave me a simple budget to follow. He told me to pay half of the smallest bill first. Once that was paid off, I was to use the extra money toward the next smallest bill and do the same until all the debt was gone. Then we were told not to use credit cards again until we were able to fit them into a budget and pay them off within the month that we used them.

We were able to pay off $50,000.00 of debt in six months. The Lord also provided a well-paying job with benefits for my husband, and I opened the Christian day care during the following year.

We now are able to tithe, give freely to ministries, help out friends and family when they need it. What took some spiritual muscles to develop is now instinctual to my husband and me.

Chapter 8

So How Important Is It That We Have a Good Root Stock?

The next stage of growth in some plants is the rootstock. If you were to buy a tree at the nursery, you would buy it during the first few years so that the root ball would not be too large. If you bought it in the first or second year, you would be buying it at the rootstock stage. It looks like it is basically a twig coming out of the root system, but not much else. But it is so much more.

The rootstock determines certain characteristics for a tree as it grows; this includes its size of maturity along with its tolerance of both water and cold weather. A rootstock is the part of the plant, often the underground part, from which new above-ground growth can be produced. It could also be described as a stem with a well-developed or well-established healthy root system to which a bud from another plant is grafted into.

A rootstock is purposely selected for its interaction with the soil. It provides the roots and the stem support for the new plant, with the ability to obtain the necessary minerals, water, and soil and resist the pests and diseases that may intend to damage it.

Grafted Into a Good Rootstock

As I have pondered how the "the apple" dream can come to fruition, I am keenly aware that we must be grafted into a good rootstock. Jesus is our rootstock! We must be grafted into the true vine or, in this case, the strong, sturdy, well-developed established root. If the rootstock in a tree determines its size of maturity, then what does Jesus, our Rootstock, determine about our maturity? As we will see, everyone matures at a different rate. The Sower knows what we need each season to produce the harvest He intended.

First, we need to be firmly established in truth, and the truth that we must be grounded in is the Good News that while we were dead in our sins, Jesus died for us! There was a meeting in heaven before the world was ever created, and in this meeting, Father, Son, and Spirit spoke of you and me and the choices that we would make, having been given free will. They knew we would blow our opportunity to do what was right in God's eyes and that we could not and would not ever meet His standard. So, they developed a plan and put it into action. They together decided that the Son of God (Jesus) would come to earth in the body that the Father had fashioned for Him. He would live and walk among us and show us the love, patience, mercy, justice, obedience, and the power of God the Father to save us. This would and could bring us into a relationship with Him (God the Father) through our faith in Jesus' life, death, and resurrection and give us the ability through His Spirit to be like Him. And even more precious is the fact that Jesus will return for us to live with Him forever.

How good is that news that the Godhead thought of you before the world was even created? I do not know about you, but that brings me great comfort and a sense that maybe, just maybe, they know what they are doing, and I can trust in their wisdom for my life! Let the union take place!

What Is Grafting Anyway?

I found this operation of grafting remarkably interesting. First, most fruit trees that are bought commercially are almost always grafted. There are two parts needed for a grafting: the first is the rootstock, and the second is called a scion. The rootstock is a part of a plant. It is usually the underground part where new above-ground growth can be produced. The rootstock is selected for its adaptability and resistance to diseases.

The scion is a piece of a young stem or bud that is inserted into a rootstock. The scion is the plant (or, in our illustration, us) that has the properties that the propagator (God) desires above ground, which would include the fruit and the ability to absorb sunlight (the Gospel) and turn it into energy. In other words, we have within us what God wants to use or display to others as He grows us to maturity, and He knows what it will take to develop us.

After the scion has been fused to the tree, the tissue of the two plants will grow together and eventually form a single plant! What is amazing about this is that after several years, it may be difficult to detect where the graft had even taken place, so much so that one may not be able to see the site of the graft. And even though the new tree always contains the components of two genetically different trees, they are one and have formed a new tree or species. And now, because of the fusion, the possibly weaker tree is almost guaranteed to be stronger, produce a better product, and be more suited to its environment.

Do you get what this is saying? When we are grafted into Jesus, we become one with Him, and we take on His characteristics so that people see the new person that we have become instead of the weak wild tree we could have been.

I also love that Jesus is adaptable and is able to resist things that would harm Him. When He becomes fully entwined in our lives, we, too, can become more adaptable and are more able to resist things that would harm us.

Also, although people see Jesus' life living through us, we are still fully human and now fully God-filled. We become a new creation or, for the sake of the illustration, a new species.

Personally, I am very aware of who I am and who I was before I became one with Jesus. It was a pretty sad picture. But by the grace of God and my walk with Jesus, people are shocked when they hear who I was and how I behaved prior to my grafting. Now, they see Jesus more than they see me. But I am still very aware of who I am apart from Christ and who is shining out and making me look good when those times are manifested.

Also, did you catch an important word...eventually? We need time to grow into the likeness of Jesus. It is not automatic, and it does not happen overnight or in one season. It is a gradual process, and our security is that we are fused together, or as Scripture puts it, we are "sealed" with the Holy Spirit. So, we can relax, trust God, and let it happen naturally.

Ephesians 1:13–14 reads:

In Him you also trusted, after you heard the word of truth, the gospel of your salvation; in whom also, having believed, you were sealed with the Holy Spirit of promise, who is given as a pledge of our inheritance, with a view to the redemption of God's own possession, to the praise of His glory.

Ephesians 1:13–14 (NKJV)

In other words, the Godhead is not going to stop working and producing in us what is needed for our maturity.

CHAPTER 9

Good Soil Needs Good Nutrients

The stage of growth that happens next, the leafy growth stage, needs something particularly important. It needs the correct nutrients for the tree to grow and mature and bear good fruit. We need water and nutrients all along the way, but now we want to see some outward growth of the rootstock. And in order to have good growth, the tree needs to be fertilized.

The Sower, when He sows the seed, will put it in good soil to make sure the correct nutrients are there to support life and growth. But as it grows, it needs some added nutrients because the soil can only hold so much at a time, and the tree has been feeding off it since its inception. We need to be feeding on the Word daily and giving it out as God directs us. Second Timothy 4:2 (NLT) reminds us to *"Preach the Word of God. Be prepared, whether the time is favorable or not. Patiently correct, rebuke, and encourage your people with good teaching."*

Can you start to see that the nutrients are used by the tree to survive, grow, and fertilize? It is needed for healthy growth, development, and functioning. But, if we add the wrong mixture of fertilizer, we will not get the correct results.

For instance, one year, I put fertilizer that I had found in my basement on some plants and wondered why I never really saw any vegetables, just lots of leaves. When I pointed it out to my brother, who is a gardener, he told me I used the wrong fertilizer, and the combination in that particular package was for an altogether different plant.

The apple tree needs potassium, nitrogen, and phosphorus in the correct proportion to grow properly, produce good fruit and stay healthy. These nutrients are found in good fertilizers and in the correct proportions needed for the individual plant or tree.

I believe, as co-laborers with God, we have the responsibility to add the right fertilizer to young believers. By this, I mean we need to teach the Word of God correctly and proportionately: not too much grace that we never ask God to search our hearts, not being so fixated on the law so that we condemn ourselves and others, and never see the payment Jesus paid on the cross for our forgiveness. Also, we are not to use our faith as an excuse to keep from doing the works that God calls us to do; those works that show that we are His children and that He is loving, generous, and merciful. Lastly, we should have enough faith to believe that God is a God of miracles: the same yesterday, today, and forever.

As I have been studying the growth of the tree and making comparisons, as I read the nutrients on the bag of fertilizer one year, I found that nitrogen helps encourage leaves and branches, phosphorus encourages root and blossom development, and potassium/potash is responsible for the apple tree's natural disease resistance and systems that support the overall health of the tree.

But did you notice the wording? Two of the nutrients were to encourage, but one was responsible. We, as believers, can encourage other believers, but God is ultimately responsible to protect us and grow us into the likeness of Christ! Jesus is the Author and Finisher of our faith.

When to Fertilize?

Do you know when you can tell if a tree needs an extra boost of fertilizer? If your new tree fails to grow at least eight to twelve inches of new green growth within a year, then it is time to fertilize it.

Can you tell when Christians have a need to be fertilized? It is when we see them becoming confused and not understanding what the Word says, and we watch them start pulling away, or when they are consistently worried or depressed and are struggling to live the life that they think is expected of them!

Worse, it is when they feel ashamed of their past and think they are not good enough to be around other believers. Or when they think that they do not have enough faith, so they go searching for answers that lead them to bad theology. To me, the hardest situation to watch is when someone thinks that God is mad at them and is punishing them because they cannot live up to His standard.

This last example breaks my heart. God redirects us by His Word and His love. We are changed by the renewing of our minds. And it is the goodness of God that leads us to repentance! It all starts on the inside, not the outside, and not by our performance. Jesus took our punishment, and God's wrath and anger were put on Jesus at the cross. He has done the work for us; we just need to rest in His finished work and realize that part of grace is the divine influence upon the heart and its reflection in our life.

The question is, do we help struggling brothers and sisters by feeding them the proper Word that they need, or do we harm them by heaping on rules or condemnation or even false hope? When we are not sensitive to the True Gardner's blend of fertilizer, or if we think we know better than the Owner of the tree, we may do more damage than help.

Even in a tree, there are seasons of growth, rest, pruning, and harvest, so do not panic but instead, give your sister or brother time to understand what life with Christ is like. Each of us must have time to get acclimated to our environment. And each of us will have seasons of noticeable growth and times that God will call us aside to rest. There will be times when He will prune us by taking something out of our lives that we may no longer need or that will harm us in the long run. And there will be times of harvest when we will share the fruits with others that He has produced in us. Believe me, for some of us, this life is way different than the life we lived before being grafted in, and if you do not understand how God works, you may become confused or discouraged when you enter into one of these seasons.

We Are Maturing but Still Need Some Help!

So now, back to our illustration, our little sapling is on its way to maturity. We have seen it grow from roots to sturdy trunk to limbs with lots of green leaves. We have watched as its trunk has grown to support branches. We know that the root system is developing because our tree is strong and healthy. We may now start to see in the springtime as the weather starts to get warmer, some leaf buds unfold, and flower buds begin to grow and may even get a little fruit after pollination.

But wait, what is pollination, and why do we need it? Simply put...it is the process of the flower becoming fruit with the help of an outside source. The process in nature has many different components that work together to produce good fruit. The process of pollination is necessary to produce seeds with surrounding fruit and to produce the next generation. Pollination is not from the tree's effort on its own, but in fact, it needs something or someone to help in the process. In nature, the tree or flower needs help from an animal, an insect, a person, a bird, or the wind to pollinate.

The tree already has the budding flower on it to attract the outside source to help complete the process. We, at this point in our spiritual walk, already have the beauty and attractiveness of God united to our spirit. And now we have the privilege of sharing with others what God is and has been doing in our lives which would help to pollinate others. We, with our spiritual gifts, have the privilege and responsibility to spread the Good News of Jesus to others. We, as followers of Jesus, are commissioned to tell others of our experiences with Him and to share our burdens with each other so we can all grow and mature together. We are also to care for one another in tangible ways. This would be called cross-pollination in nature.

Common Pollinators

I often see bees and hummingbirds at my fruit trees; they are common pollinators. In our spiritual life, we already have the fruit of the Holy Spirit in our spirit, but we need it to come forth so others may take of it. Sometimes we need help to be pollinated so that we produce the good fruit, which is the image of Christ in us.

The Holy Spirit has already been doing the work in us, but God, by His grace, has invited us to be a part of each other's life. When we are angry or discouraged or hurting, the Holy Spirit sends us the Word that we need through either the Scriptures themselves as we meditate on them or through another person. This can come from the scriptures being revealed to you personally. It can come from a sermon; it can come from another person, church, or organization ministering to you. God knows how to get to us what we need, and in the time He has appointed it. When the truth is received, then you will manifest love, peace, joy, longsuffering, gentleness, goodness, faith, meekness, and temperance.

In our spiritual life, we have the Holy Spirit and people to carry the Word, which is in our spirit, to our soul, which is our heart, mind, and will, so the seed (the Word) can start to produce fruit around it. This is one of God's mysteries. We cannot explain it, and we need not try.

Ephesians 4:15–16 tells us,

Instead, speaking the truth in love, we will grow to become in every respect the mature body of him who is the head, that is, Christ. From him the whole body, joined and held together by every supporting ligament, grows and builds itself up in love, as each part does its work.

Ephesians 4:15–16 (NIV)

We also read in John 3:8 (NIV), "The wind blows wherever it pleases. You hear its sound but cannot tell where it comes from or where it is going. So, it is with everyone born of the Spirit."

In Acts 2:1–4, we see the Holy Spirit at work, and He comes as a wind. It reads:

When the Day of Pentecost had fully come, they were all with one accord in one place. And suddenly there came a sound from heaven, as of a rushing mighty wind, and

it filled the whole house where they were

sitting. Then there appeared to them divided

tongues, as of fire, and one sat upon each of

them. And they were all filled with the Holy

Spirit and began to speak with other tongues,

as the Spirit gave them utterance.

Acts 2:1–4 (NKJV)

The Spirit Enables Us to Speak

When we read the above verses, we see that the Holy Spirit appeared to sit upon each of the disciples. Once they were filled with the Holy Spirit, they were able to speak as the Spirit gave them utterance. Notice they did not speak whatever they wanted to but what the Spirit enabled them to say.

Have you ever been with someone or in a group of people, and there is a discussion taking place, and you felt this sense down in your stomach to say something, but you were extremely uncomfortable to do so? Maybe you thought you would be talked over, or maybe you would be moving the discussion in another direction that those listening may not approve of, or maybe you felt you were not as spiritually mature as the others. Whatever the reason, you did not want to speak, and yet as the conversation continued, so did the prompting in your spirit grow louder and stronger until it just burst out of you. You can thank the Holy Spirit for that! He knows what needs to be said, and He gives you the ability to say it. I have had this experience many times in my life, and I do not always get a positive reaction, but I know that the Lord knows why it was said to that person or group of people, and it is His Spirit at work changing hearts and minds.

I have also had times when I have said something that I had not even thought of, and yet it came out of my mouth, and it was exactly what the other person needed to hear, and it was in line with what they had been praying about, and yet I had no idea of any of it. The best experience for me is when the Holy Spirit reveals a nugget of truth to me personally, and I get to share it with others. Some of the time, I am hearing it for the first time as I am speaking it out to others. I can honestly testify that when I need God to help me, He is there either by His Word, His Spirit, or a person, and my faith and my fruit mature as a result.

So, who or what is the pollinator of your fruit? Is it the Holy Spirit working through the Word or another person? If it is, then you will produce love, joy, peace, patience, kindness, goodness, faithfulness, gentleness, and self-control. God's Spirit is like the wind. We receive the Holy Spirit with our salvation. He enters our hearts the moment we make the conscious decision to follow Jesus and let Him be the Lord of our lives and is continually working in our lives and those around us.

Sealed with the Holy Spirit

There is another part of the pollination process, it not only produces the seed and the fruit, but in an apple, it creates a protective barrier around the seed. Did you know that all seeds are protected by a coat? We, as Christ believers, are sealed with the Holy Spirit, and He protects the incorruptible seed, which is the truth that has been pollinated in us. Ephesians 1:13 (NKJV) tells us, "In Him you also trusted after you heard the word of truth, the Gospel of your salvation; in whom also, having believed, ye were sealed with the Holy Spirit of promise."

There are also different reasons that we see the Spirit being imparted on the disciples. One of these times is when Jesus spoke of imparting the Holy Spirit on the disciples in John 20:21–23,

> **So Jesus said to them again, "Peace to you! As the Father has sent Me, I also send you." And when He had said this, He breathed on them, and said to them, "Receive the Holy Spirit. If you forgive the sins of any, they are forgiven them; if you retain the sins of any, they are retained."**
>
> **John 20:21–23 (NKJV)**

These verses are so precious because Jesus was inviting them to not only preach of what they had seen and heard of Him, but He was telling them that whoever believed their message could be assured that their sins were forgiven. And those who rejected Jesus could be certain that their sins were not forgiven. Once we come to faith in Jesus' finished work on the cross and have been anointed with the Holy Spirit of God, we also can assure others of their salvation and security of forgiveness of sins when they accept Jesus' payment for their sins and put their faith in Him.

Later Jesus told the 120 disciples to wait until the anointing of the Spirit at Pentecost, which gave power to the disciples. Prior to the Holy Spirit anointing on them, the disciples were told by Jesus to wait. But once they were filled, they went throughout the region, bringing the good news to all who would accept it.

While being together and eating with them, He commanded them not to leave Jerusalem, but to wait for what the Father had promised, "Of which," He said, "you have heard Me speak. For John baptized with water, but you will be baptized and empowered and united with the Holy Spirit, not long from now."

Acts 1:4–5 (AMP)

Again, in verse 8, Jesus tells them,

But you will receive power and ability when the Holy Spirit comes upon you; and you will be My witnesses [to tell people about Me] both in Jerusalem and in all Judea, and Samaria, and even to the ends of the earth.

Acts 1:8 (AMP)

This Pentecost event was associated with being baptized, being fully immersed in, empowered by, and united with the Spirit of God so that they could be Jesus' witnesses to the world. This experience only required the disciples to believe Jesus and to wait where He told them to wait. They believed Jesus, and the proof was that they waited. Then in the appointed time (God's timing), the Holy Spirit came anointing them with power.

What a precious gift we have been given. I wonder how many people have been fully immersed in the Spirit and empowered to be Jesus' witnesses?

There is a beautiful story of how the Holy Spirit brought life to not only Mary and Joseph but ultimately to us.

Luke 1:30–35, 38 tells us:

But the angel said to her, "Do not be afraid, Mary; you have favor with God. You will conceive and give birth to a son, and you are to call him Jesus. He will be great and will be called the Son of the Most High. The Lord God will give him the throne of his father David, and he will reign over Jacob's descendants forever; his kingdom will never end."

"How will this be," Mary asked the angel,

"since I am a virgin?"

The angel answered, "The Holy Spirit will

come on you, and the power of the Most

High will overshadow you. So, the holy one

to be born will be called the Son of God."

"I am the Lord's servant," Mary answered.

"May your word to me be fulfilled." Then the

angel left her.

Luke 1:30–35, 38 (NIV)

Did you catch what was said? The holy life that the angel was talking about was conceived by the Holy Spirit and brought through a person. That same life or, in our comparison, "fruit" is also brought about by the Holy Spirit as we believe and in belief say "yes" to His promptings. We do not need angels to speak to us today; we have the Spirit living in us, and the fruit that we are hoping to produce is only possible because God chose a person (Mary) to carry His Seed (Jesus), and that Seed grew up amongst us.

The Tender Green Shoot

Isaiah 53:2 tells us about Jesus as a man:

In God's eyes he was like a tender green shoot, sprouting from a root in dry and sterile ground. But in our eyes there was no attractiveness at all, nothing to make us want him.

Isaiah 53:2 (TLB)

I am so glad that God allowed Jesus to be that "tender green shoot, sprouting from a root in dry and sterile ground." Jesus is alive and growing His life in mine, even though I had dry and sterile ground for Him to grow in.

Our question now is, are you aware that He has pollinated you? Do you sense that He is touching those tender, intimate areas of your heart so that good fruit can be produced? If you have, you will start to see the fruit grow. But the tree does not grow a large crop all at once; even this takes time. The first few years of growth may only produce a few apples.

We see the same in our spiritual life; we do not produce all of the fruit of the Spirit in a single season. Nor do different varieties of fruit trees produce fruit at the same rate of time.

I have different fruit trees in my yard, including a cherry tree. I actually cut down my first cherry tree because I thought it was damaged and nonproductive. I had thought this because my other trees, the apples, and the peach tree, which I planted at the same time as the cherry tree, were producing fruit.

When I realized after several years that my second cherry tree was not producing, I went to my computer to try to find out why. Guess what I read? A cherry tree, unlike an apple or peach tree, takes seven to ten years to produce fruit. I sadly realized that I mistakenly cut down my tree before it was ever possible to produce its fruit. I wonder how many people we "cut down" before God is ready for their fruit to appear.

CHAPTER 10

Seasonal Fruit Growth Has Enemies

Are you also aware that each new season after the tree starts to produce fruit, some of it will fall off the tree or be stolen? My trees have a great amount of fruit at the beginning of the season. But there are many enemies that cause my fruit to fall or disappear during each new growing season.

> ➤ In nature, animals eat the unripe fruit, especially when they sense a different weather pattern.

> ➤ Storms will displace some.

> ➤ At times, a simple wind at the correct angle will cause some fruit to fall.

> ➤ I have even seen birds eat apples and cherries off my tree.

> ➤ And without fail, bugs attack the unripe fruit.

Now let us remember, this will not stop the tree from producing more fruit next season, and it may cause some of the other fruit to grow larger and sweeter as the season goes on. What is happening is different from the seed falling on bad soil or being choked out by weeds. Our seed has been producing, and we have been growing, but now something is stopping it from its full harvest.

Have you sensed this in your life? If so, you can relax. God is constantly growing us and bringing us into new seasons of life, both naturally and spiritually. And in the beginning of each new season, we face obstacles that may make us feel as though we are not producing any fruit. But if we are truly God's children, we will produce the fruit of His Spirit.

> ➤ Our fruit of the Spirit is love, joy, peace, longsuffering (patience), goodness, faithfulness, meekness (gentleness), and temperance (self-control). This fruit is in us because the Spirit is in us. It is His fruit being manifested through our knowledge of Jesus and our recognition of who we are in Christ. Just like the tree is growing fruit that grew from the seed, the fruit in us is now growing by the power of the Spirit.

Let us first look at some of the ways the owner of the orchard handles these obstacles.

> ➤ In the apple orchards, I have seen the owner hire men to spray pesticides on the trees to keep the bugs from destroying the crop. (God is the owner of the orchard, and we are the ones who help others from being destroyed by covering others in prayer and by encouraging other believers during a difficult season.)

> ➤ I have also seen the trees being planted close together and in specific locations for the best advantage from the elements and for cross-pollination. (We are placed with other believers in churches and small groups. We also have the Spirit of God living in us and the Word of God near us for our growth, so when storms come our way, we do not have to face them alone.)

> ➤ The irrigation is done from below, so it does not discolor the apples and leave spots on them. (The Spirit of God waters us, we are told that it springs up in us.)

➤ Fences are used to keep larger animals out, and a dead animal on the fence is a warning to any predators that might think they could have a free lunch. (Boundaries are needed for our protection.)

➤ And a really interesting method of keeping the fruit safe is to wrap each piece of fruit individually or in small clumps in bags to keep them safe. (We are hidden in Christ Jesus.)

Psalm 27:1–5 speaks of this,

The LORD is my light and my salvation; whom shall I fear? the LORD is the strength of my life; of whom shall I be afraid? When the wicked, even mine enemies and my foes, came upon me to eat my flesh, they stumbled and fell. Though an host should encamp against me, my heart shall not fear: though war shall rise against me, in this will I be confident. One thing have I desired of the LORD, that I will seek after; that I may dwell in the house of the Lord all the days of my life, to behold the beauty of the LORD, and to enquire in his temple. For in the time of

trouble he shall hide me in his pavilion: in the secret of his tabernacle shall he hide me; he shall set me up upon a rock.

Psalm 27:1–5 (KJV)

Those Pesky Bugs

In all of our lives, there are those pesky bugs. Those trivial things that irritate us. Those situations that do not seem to go away; they just keep popping up when and where you least expect them. They rob us of our peace and our joy.

Most of us have habits that annoy us, anger us, or disappoint us, or we have others around us that do it to us. We do not want to be irritated, but we find that we are. Why is this? It is usually because we have a higher expectation of ourselves or others than we should. We want perfection, comfort, and convenience. This is when we need others to cover us in prayer and encourage us to look to the Word for admonishment. This is also a time when we need to speak truth into each other so our minds can be transformed according to God's Word.

On our trees, in the spring, there are these little black spots that are barely visible to see unless you know what you are looking for. But as the season progresses, these spots start to grow and turn into hungry leaf-eating larvae that can cause havoc on our fruit trees.

Just as these bugs need to be removed from our trees, so do our negative thoughts need to be removed from our minds. When we do not catch our comments or thoughts while they are still small, they can grow into an extremely dangerous enemy that can steal our fruit and destroy what is growing around us.

God has said we would have trouble and tribulation but be of good cheer, for He has overcome the world. So how do we keep the Spirit's fruit from disappearing?

Romans 12:2 tells us,

Do not be conformed to this world [its thinking], but be transformed by the renewing of your mind, that you may prove what is that good and acceptable and perfect will of God.

Romans 12:2 (NKJV)

When was the last time you thought about how wonderful your supposed adversary has been to you at other times? Have you ever stopped to look at the situation with an unfamiliar perspective, one that reveals the truth in a new way? And do you see yourself as God sees you, clothed with the righteousness of Jesus?

Philippians 4:8 (NIV) tells us how to keep the fruit of peace, joy, and even patience and long-suffering...

Finally, brothers and sisters, whatever is true, whatever is noble, whatever is right, whatever is pure, whatever is lovely, whatever

is admirable—if anything is excellent and

praiseworthy—think about such things.

Philippians 4:8 (NIV)

Have you ever told the enemy to get out of your head, and instead, you spoke of how much God loves you and rejoiced in the truth of who you are in Christ? Do you realize that God sees you as being righteous in Christ? Also, have you ever stopped and considered why you are angry? Could it be that you are afraid for yourself or someone else? Fear and anger go hand in hand with each other. When we see sin in our lives or the lives of those we love or respect, we tend to become angry. Why is this? Is it because we do not believe that God in His grace can transform the sinner? Do we expect ourselves and others to change on our own or their own and with natural strength? Do we stop and pray for the Spirit of God to start working in our or their lives in these situations? Do we bring the Word of truth to our minds or to them?

No matter the situation, we cannot let those negative thoughts keep buzzing around our minds. They are lies from the enemy. Second Corinthians 10:4–5 tells us,

(For the weapons of our warfare are not

carnal, but mighty through God to the

pulling down of strong holds;)

Casting down imaginations, and every

high thing that exalteth itself against the

knowledge of God, and bringing into captivity every thought to the obedience of Christ;

2 Corinthians 10:4–5 (KJV)

This verse is not talking about our obedience but that we should consider Jesus' obedience to the Father's will and what He has done for us. So, instead of thinking of the sin or failure, spend time renewing your mind. Instead of reminding yourself how much you are annoyed, angry, or disappointed, think on the things God tells us to think on. Better yet, speak or sing about what is good, lovely, and pure, the things that Jesus has done for us and has provided to us. I love to change my mind by singing and worshipping God. It is amazing how your perspective changes when you focus on the goodness of God! Then I am able to go to prayer and hear God's voice over the situation.

Remind yourself that the fruit that wants to come forth takes some effort on our part. According to Ephesians 4:2 (NIV), **we must be completely humble and gentle; be patient, bearing with one another in love.**

Ask the Lord to show you how to be humble and learn to love as Jesus loved us. When we stay in tune with the Spirit, He will change your heart and mind, cleansing you when you need to be cleansed and redirecting your thoughts and actions if you will allow Him to.

And if we find that God has put us in a situation where we see sin in another person's life, Galatians 6:1 (NIV) instructs us, "Brothers and sister, if someone is caught in a sin, you who live by the Spirit should restore that person gently. But watch yourselves, or you may be tempted."

Wouldn't it be great if we just needed to have some head

knowledge of scripture? Well, some people think that knowledge alone works (read a verse once or hear a sermon), but that is not true. We are told to meditate on the Word. We are told to not be hearers only but doers of the word.

The truth is that what you need is already placed in your spirit by the Holy Spirit; He has come into your life, He has sealed you unto salvation, and He has been at work transforming your life. But you need to cooperate with Him by reading the Word, studying the Word, and letting it have a place in your heart so that the faith that God has placed in you can bring life to you, which is called believing. When we come to believing the Word (which means to be in agreement with the Word and to have it so real to us that no one can snatch the truth from us) and submit ourselves to His promptings, we will see the manifestation of the changed heart and mind.

The Storms of Life

When I think of the storms of life, I am reminded of the wise and foolish builders found in Matthew 7:24–27:

"Therefore everyone who hears these words

of mine and puts them into practice is like

a wise man who built his house on the rock.

The rain came down, the streams rose,

and the winds blew and beat against the

house; yet it did not fall, because it had its

foundation on the rock. But everyone who

hears these words of mine and does not put

them into practice is like a foolish man who

built his house on sand. The rain came down,

the streams rose, and the winds blew and

beat

against that house, and it fell with a great

crash."

Matthew 7:24–27 (NIV)

All of us have storms in our lives, it might be illness, loss of a job or business, or a family member, and those are just a few examples. So, what did Jesus say about keeping things together? He said everyone who hears these words and puts them into practice is like a wise man. James speaks of it this way...

But be ye doers of the word, and not hearers

only, deceiving your own selves.

For if any be a hearer of the word, and not

a doer, he is like unto a man beholding his

natural face in a glass:

143

For he beholdeth himself, and goeth his way, and straightway forgetteth what manner of man he was.

James 1:22–24 (KJV)

The storms in life will be ineffective when we listen to the Spirit for the Word of God above the circumstances of the storm and let Him direct our attitude, our emotions, and our behaviors. In other words, do what He instructs you to do!

Have you ever noticed that when a storm comes, you seem to forget about everything else and just focus on the impending doom? Even in a natural storm, we prepare our house, purchase supplies ahead of time, check to make sure everything is fully charged, get out the candles, and put gas in the generator.

So why are we so unprepared for our spiritual storms? Maybe because we do not take the Word of God so seriously. Maybe we do not really think that there is a spiritual world all around us, actively seeking to destroy our lives, our families, and our ministries. Or maybe we are just lazy, thinking we do not really have to be prepared. Well, unfortunately, the unprepared may realize that we are more dependent on the people picking the fruit than the vine itself. If this is so, we may become bruised or damaged.

I had a friend who was a young Christian and new to our church. Her husband owned his own company, and they were successful. She was well-liked by the leadership and was soon put into a position of authority herself. Unfortunately, the fruit in her was not fully ripe yet.

Soon a storm arose when one of her parents died, and when the overflowing emotions came into her life, she did not know enough or maybe have the strength to rely on the Spirit within her for comfort. She had expectations of those around her to comfort her and be there for her. Sadly, she did not feel supported in her time of distress. The people she thought would show up for the funeral did not. She left the church and the positions that she had held. She fell out of fellowship with the people who had befriended her and put her into those positions. She did not lose her relationship with Jesus—it was damaged but not destroyed.

Sadly, this happened to my dad also. He expected certain people to be there for him when his mom died, but they were not. This left a bitter taste in his mouth for years. Mercy and encouragement are gifts of the Spirit, and when we do not have the whole community using their gifts properly, some of our fruit gets bruised.

But thankfully, Jesus knew that we would not always be enough for each other. Remember, He spent three years with His disciples, and they constantly had trouble encouraging each other. So, Jesus sent His Spirit to live in us.

If you love Me, keep My commandments.

And I will pray the Father, and He will give

you another Helper [the Spirit] that He may

abide with you forever—the Spirit of truth,

whom the world cannot receive, because it

neither sees Him nor knows Him; but you

know Him, for He dwells with you and will be in you. I will not leave you orphans; I will come to you.

John 14:15–18 (NKJV)

Praise be to the God and Father of our Lord Jesus Christ, the Father of compassion and the God of all comfort, who comforts us in all our troubles, so that we can comfort those in any trouble with the comfort we ourselves receive from God.

2 Corinthians 1:3–4 (NIV)

Romans 10:8 is a great reminder of why we should memorize scripture. It reads, "But what does it say? 'The word is near you; it is in your mouth and in your heart,' that is, the message concerning faith that we proclaim" (Romans 10:8, NIV).

One of the ways that we see that our fruit is truly growing is when we are able to comfort others in their time of need. Romans 12:15 (NIV) reminds us to "Rejoice with those who rejoice, mourn with those who mourn."

We all know that the storms will come, but do we really believe that we do not need to be moved by them? We get to remind ourselves that we are like eagles that fly above the storms looking down at them; remember, we are seated in heavenly places.

I remember when my dad died, the day after his funeral, I was in church, and we were singing a song with a line that said, "I have a father." I burst into tears right there in the middle of the song. I was so overtaken with grief that I fell back into the chair. Then I heard that beautiful, still small voice in my spirit that rose to my mind. He said to me, "You have a Father." God was assuring me through His Spirit that I did indeed have a living Father. I was not fatherless just because my earthly father had passed on into his home in glory. I was able to stand back up and sing with tears in my eyes, but now those tears were of joy mixed with the grief.

Never, and I will say it again, never forget what Jesus paid for you to experience the love, favor, and comfort of God in your life. When we call on Him in the midst of the storm, He hears us and comes quickly to rescue us. As our fruit grows, we will recognize His voice and learn to trust it so that we do not have to always be looking for others to meet our emotional needs.

But we must believe His Word and be listening and expecting not only His Word of wisdom and love, but we must be willing to respond in faith, which means to agree with Him and therefore do as He instructs us to do. Remember, grace has already provided everything we need, and we receive it by faith. Our obedience springs from within us because God has given us a new heart and, with it, new desires. This is how we stay on the vine and grow. We go from faith to faith, which means God keeps giving us His desires, and the more we respond correctly, the more we see how faithful He is, and it gives us the ability to trust Him more.

It is good to have friends to support and comfort us during the storms of our life, and we are instructed by God to comfort each other and uphold each other. But we must also learn that there are times when we need to take quiet refuge in Him alone. Unfortunately, I have seen so many times when people, including myself, look to others before looking to God to find our encouragement. And because we are focused on the situation rather than on the goodness of God, we lose our peace, our joy, our faithfulness, and maybe even our self-control.

Jesus Provides Our Living Water!

We have already seen that the seed needs a good dose of water to start the growth process, but that initial watering will not be enough to support the plant, flower, or tree for the rest of its life. The flower, plant, or tree needs a continual flow of water.

We, as Christ-followers, also need a continual flow of Living Water. And Jesus is the provider of that water. In John 7:37–39, we read,

On the last day, that great day of the feast, Jesus stood and cried out, saying, "If anyone thirst, let him come to Me and drink. He who believes in Me, as the Scripture has said, out of his heart will flow rivers of living water." But this He spoke concerning the Spirit, whom those believing in Him would receive; for the Holy Spirit was not yet given, because Jesus was not yet glorified.

John 7:37–39 (NKJV)

Jesus assures us that once we come to believe in Him because He has been glorified, we will have the Spirit living in us. This water will not only sustain us, but it will spring up to everlasting life. John 4:13–14 tells us this truth,

> **Jesus answered and said to her, "Whoever drinks of this water will thirst again, but whoever drinks of the water that I shall give him will never thirst. But the water I shall give him will become in him a fountain of water springing up into everlasting life."**
>
> **John 4:13–14 (NKJV)**

What Do We Know of the Spirit?

Our fruit would not survive on a parched half-dead tree, and we cannot and would not keep our spiritual fruit growing and being sustained without the work of the Holy Spirit. When we think of the Spirit's work in our lives, we will notice several aspects of His ministry.

> ➤ He is our comforter and teacher, "But the Comforter, which is the Holy Ghost, whom the Father will send in my name, he shall teach you all things, and bring remembrance, whatsoever I have said unto you" (John 14:26, KJV).

> ➤ He is the power in us that gives us boldness to be witnesses

for Jesus. "But you shall receive power when the Holy Spirit has come upon you; and you shall be witnesses to Me in Jerusalem, and in all Judea and Samaria, and to the end of the earth" (Acts 1:8, NKJV).

➤ He is our guide, "However, when He, the Spirit of truth, has come, He will guide you into all truth; for He will not speak on His own authority, but whatever He hears He will speak; and He will tell you things to come" (John 16:13, NKJV).

➤ He will bring unity to the believers, "Now the multitude of those who believed were of one heart and one soul; neither did anyone say that any of the things he possessed was his own, but they had all things in common" (Acts 4:32, NKJV).

➤ He leads us, "For as many as are led by the Spirit of God, these are the sons of God" (Romans 8:14, NKJV).

➤ He convicts, "Nevertheless I tell you the truth. It is to your advantage that I go away; for if I do not go away, the Helper will not come to you; but if I depart, I will send Him to you. And when He has come, He will convict the world of sin, and of righteousness, and of judgment: of sin, because they do not believe in Me; of righteousness, because I go to the Father and you see Me no more; of judgment, because the ruler of this world is judged" (John 16:7–11, NKJV).

The work of the Holy Spirit is to give us the power and ability to live the life that Jesus died for us to have. As we study the Bible, the Spirit makes Jesus' life and words come alive in us, and our hearts and mind are cleansed and nurtured. The Holy Spirit is empowering us to be more like Jesus so that our fruit is pleasing to others, so that

God may be glorified. But just as we must believe what Jesus has done for us in purchasing our salvation by dying on the cross and shedding His blood for our redemption, we must also obey the prompting of the Spirit so we do not grieve or quench the flow of the Spirit in our lives.

Ephesians 4:30–32 speaks to us this way,

And do not grieve the Holy Spirit of God, with whom you were sealed for the day of redemption. Get rid of all bitterness, rage and anger, brawling and slander, along with every form of malice. Be kind and compassionate to one another, forgiving each, just as in Christ God forgave you.

Ephesians 4:30–32 (NIV)

"Quench not the Spirit" (1 Thessalonians 5:19, KJV). In other words, do not stifle the Holy Spirit from working in your life.

Are you allowing the Holy Spirit to be the life-giving water that wells up inside of you and does the work of sanctification in your life? To be sanctified is to be set apart for special use or purpose. It is through the process that the Holy Spirit wants to do in your life, so you are equipped to do that which God has chosen and called you to do for the kingdom of God.

Chapter 11

Boundaries Protect

But how do we, as the children of God, keep from losing all of our fruit as we enter a new season of life or ministry? When I think of the enemy coming to steal or rob from us, as an animal in nature would do, two things come to mind: one is we need boundaries, and the other is we need Jesus' shed blood.

I have a friend who had been asked to be the point person for a ministry that she and her late husband had been involved in for years. She is a faithful member of her church and is very well known for her love of God and love for her church family.

When asked to take this position, there was an excitement and a hesitancy. So, she asked the Lord for confirmation, which He gave her by a verse of scripture, an agreement by her small group Bible study members, and a positive response from her pastor. Now she was ready to take on this assignment.

She was also assigned a woman to be part of the team that she was developing. But this woman tried to take the lead. She went about doing things as she felt she wanted them done.

My friend was being led by the Spirit and was starting to sense that something was wrong. When she spoke to me about the situation, I immediately knew what was going on because I had just come out of a similar situation that had caused me great harm.

This woman was showing behaviors that were not in line with someone who was part of a team. But instead, she was taking over and trying to set up meetings and arrange activities that had not been discussed. She was also correcting my friend in a way that made her feel uncomfortable.

In my situation, I felt I had no one to go to at the time. But in my friend's situation, we were able to identify the enemy and his tactics. And in doing so, she was able to speak to the right people at the right time, so she did not give up.

The pastors that she spoke with, one of them being the person who had asked her to take this position, made it clear that she was the point person. He also made it clear that there were specific protocols (boundaries) that must be kept by the church.

The other woman was not aware of the church's protocols, and by going in her own direction and making plans without the proper authority to do so, she would be violating those protocols.

When my friend spoke to the pastor, she asked for a meeting to discuss the chain of command, including his authority over her, and the procedures that the church would expect for different events and meetings. He assured her that he would speak to the woman and set the boundaries. He would speak to her about her responsibilities and what was allowed and not allowed at the church.

Now, I tell you this story because my friend was about to step aside. She was discouraged before the program even got off the ground. She was going to step down and yield to this other woman, giving her the responsibility of the program.

How had the enemy come in? He came in through a person whose intentions were good but misplaced. And in the behaviors shown, she was like a wolf in sheep's clothing. She was harming my friend with her words by making arrangements without consulting her and by making her feel guilty for going to the proper leadership for direction.

Let us remember that we do not fight against flesh and blood. This woman was not acting in this way to harm my friend, but by not staying under the authority of my friend or the church leadership, she was being used by the enemy, whether she realized it or not.

When I look at my friend's reaction and attitude toward this woman and the situation, I see three things.

> First, she was able to continue being the point person, and this was done by letting the Spirit lead her. He was giving her verses that led her in the right direction.

> The second safeguard was when she sought to find the boundaries, in other words, the protocols of the church; they were already in place for her to rely on.

> The third was that she surrounded herself within close proximity to other believers who are led by the Spirit. She was able to listen to their advice and was protected.

The fruit of the Spirit that shone in this situation included love, gentleness, and goodness. My friend lovingly had conversations with this woman, explaining each step of the way what she was doing and why.

But my friend was robbed of the fruit of peace. Each conversation that they had left my friend uneasy or unsettled. She also almost lost her fruit of faithfulness to what God had called her to do.

But again, the Spirit stepped in as she went to prayer, and He spoke the verse of authority to her. "Behold, I give unto you power to tread on serpents and scorpions, and over all the power of the enemy: and nothing by any means will hurt you" (Luke 10:19, KJV).

In this season of her life, God was trying to show her the authority we have in Christ Jesus. The enemy does not want us to know who we are by the power of the Spirit living us. He will always try to rob us of this truth.

First Corinthians 13:4–8 speaks of the Spirit's fruit being manifested.

Love is patient, love is kind. It does not envy, it does not boast, it is not proud. It does not dishonor others, it is not self-seeking, it is not easily angered, it keeps no record of wrongs. Love does not delight in evil but rejoices with the truth. It always protects, always trusts, always hopes, always preservers.

Love never fails.

1 Corinthians 13:4–8a (NIV)

When we let the Spirit guide our hearts and minds with the truth of the gospel, then His fruit will grow, and others will be able to enjoy it. When we are able to call on the Spirit and ask Him to show us how He would handle a situation and obey His promptings in a difficult situation, then our fruit of love, gentleness, and goodness are manifested for all to see and taste.

"O taste and see that the LORD is good: blessed is the man that trusteth in him" (Psalm 34:8, KJV).

The Dream of Protection

A few years back, I had a dream of one of my daughters and another family member being attacked by a wolf. In this dream, the two girls were playing in a field of tall grass. They were chasing each other and laughing, just being children on a bright summer day. I was happy to see them having fun, but then I saw something out of the corner of my eye. I was not sure what it was; it was about the size of an adult dog, it was low to the ground, and it was lying still. It looked as though it was watching the girls. The reason I was able to see it was because the wind blew, and it drew my attention to a tree in that direction.

Suddenly, as though out of nowhere, the animal came to life and started to run through the field straight toward them. He was growling and showing his teeth. When they saw him, they started screaming and running. He was now in pursuit of them as they were being chased through the field. It was a wolf, and he was getting closer to them. They could hear him growling at them and see him showing his teeth. The fear caused them to fall: it caused them to get some cuts and bruises. It caused them to separate from each other.

In my dream, I could see that there was a barn nearby with a fence set up to keep sheep and goats safe. It looked like a pen that you would see at a petting zoo, with a barn that had a large opening attached to it.

I became keenly aware that the wolf wanted to hurt them. I yelled to them to get into the pen, knowing that they would be safe behind the boundary of the fence. Eventually, they made it to the pen, ran in, closed the gate behind them, and stayed there. The wolf was not able to get to them or harm them.

In time both of these girls were in different situations in their real lives that were trying to destroy their lives. The enemy was speaking lies to them. His tactics were successful because of the painful situations that had taken place earlier in their individual lives. Each girl was in a new relationship. In each situation, a person was being used to separate them from their loved ones, to destroy their confidence in who they were, and to destroy the truth that they had been taught, which was that God was alive and loved them.

The enemy's words spoken to them by others led to actions that were driving them far from the family that loved them. And their reactions to the pain they were feeling, along with the lies being told to them, were harming them physically, emotionally, and spiritually.

When my daughter started to go through her situation, the Lord reminded me of the dream He had given me about the two girls. He also reminded me of His faithfulness toward me when I had been in pain and made wrong and harmful decisions. But again, I did not understand what the dream meant or what my part in the dream actually was to be. I just pushed ahead, thinking I was supposed to put up the boundaries, or better yet, I was trying to control the situation in my own strength.

Being a Christian mother, I gave her boundaries to protect her, but she did not want to go under my authority. She did not see the danger that the enemy was about to spring on her. It was not until a few months into the relationship that she started to feel the hold that this man had on her. It seemed as though the enemy had captured her, and I was unable to do anything to change the situation.

I prayed for my daughter, but at the time, I did not seem to have the wisdom to stop the attack, and I did not have enough faith or understanding that God was the one who was ultimately protecting her and would only allow the enemy to go so far in his attack. I, like any mother, reacted in a way that I thought would stop or lessen the time of her spiritual attack. Looking back, I realized that I was praying but not really listening to the quiet voice that could have directed me differently. I was too busy listening to other voices, including my own, which was not in line with God's voice.

It is funny to think of it, but even the enemy has boundaries set by God. Although it looked as though the enemy was winning the battle, God's promise of protection, God's hedge of protection, was around my daughter.

Eventually, she was freed from that harmful relationship and the man that was being used by the enemy to attempt to destroy her life, her healthy relationships, and her future.

The Lord, by His mercy, allowed my daughter to move back with us, live with us, and be healed.

I can now trust that if Jesus has begun a good work, then He will finish it. For Jesus is the author and perfector of our faith. Faith is part of the fruit of the Spirit. The enemy was trying to rob both of us of this truth.

This situation took place while my daughter was in school, and although it looked as though she would not graduate, she did. She has been diagnosed with learning disabilities but has overcome them and is able to work and make good decisions. My daughter is now engaged to a man who loves her very much.

I was very aware that in my daughter's situation, I did not handle it correctly at the time. I found that I was trying to set the boundaries for my daughter in my own strength. This accomplished nothing but push her further away.

The boundary that I was setting was not done out of love; it was done with anger, fear, resentment, and embarrassment. I was not giving her a safe place to heal and grow. Sometimes we think we are doing God's will because we know what the law tells us to do and the consequences that come from taking certain actions. In knowing or assuming the results, we try to cause someone else to live under the law. It does not work. There is a difference between a boundary and a law. A boundary protects you; it gives you the ability to keep people out and let others in.

A boundary gives you space and time to move around and be made well. It gives you time to talk with someone. It allows you space to have those emotions dealt with, and it allows you to express the pain you are feeling. It also gives you time to make wise decisions.

I cannot help but think of two scripture stories, one being of Job and how God had a hedge of protection around him so that nothing bad seemed to happen to him. Then Satan showed up while the sons of God were presenting themselves before God.

God and Satan have an interesting conversation in which Satan claims that if God would take his hedge of protection off of Job, then Job will curse God to his face. So, Satan is allowed to have a certain amount of power to see if Job will be faithful to God or not. Although calamity comes upon Job and his family, his friends accuse him, and his wife encourages him to curse God, he is able to keep himself from cursing God. But notice, during his calamity and his accusers speaking to him, God gives him time to ask questions and think about what is happening and what is being said to him. Even though it does not seem it, there is still a hedge of protection around Job, God has only allowed Satan to go so far in his attempt to destroy Job's faith in God.

The beauty of this story is that Satan loses and loses in a big way. God knew what the outcome would be for Job. All these losses, all these accusations against Job, and all his ignorant outbursts of speaking his mind led him to exactly the place that God needed him to be so that he could hear God speak. God spoke to Job after all the others had spoken their thoughts to him.

Job 42:1–6 tells us,

This was Job's reply to Yahweh:
"I know that you are all-powerful: what you
conceive, you can perform. I am the man
who obscured your designs with my empty-
headed words. I have been holding forth on
matters I cannot understand, on marvels
beyond me and my knowledge. (Listen, I
have more to say, now it is my turn to ask
questions and yours to inform me.) I knew
you then only by hearsay; but now, having
seen you with my own eyes, I retract all I have
said, and in dust and ashes I repent."

Job 42:1–6 (NJB)

God opened Job's eyes to see Him in a new and more personal way. And then He was able to bless him. God knows how to hedge us in and when to let the enemy test us. Through these experiences, we usually come to a deeper understanding of God.

The second story that comes to mind is Peter. Jesus tells him that Satan has asked him to sift him as wheat. This means that Satan wanted to shake Peter's faith and cause him to fall. Just as he had hoped to do to Job, it looks as though Peter did not fare so well in his testing.

But this is where the beauty comes in; the accuser or adversary, which is what his name means, can only go so far. And although Peter did not stand as he hoped and claimed he would. Jesus had assured him that He had pleaded in prayer for Peter, that his faith should not fail.

Jesus is our high priest that prays for us. He is the one who speaks to God on our behalf. God always listens to Jesus because God sees Jesus as righteous and Holy. Jesus' prayer caused that hedge of protection to be around Peter so that he would not lose his faith and therefore not lose his relationship with Jesus.

There is a difference between committing a sin and losing your faith and love for Jesus. And we know that Peter was protected because after Jesus rose again, He went to Peter personally and spoke words of confirmation and gave him the instruction to feed Jesus' sheep.

At the time, it seemed as though there was not a hedge of protection around my daughter, but there was; in fact, she came to have a deeper relationship with us, and we have had some particularly good conversations about Jesus, who He is and how He works in our lives. She sees Jesus differently now than before she went through her difficulties. God does not always keep what we call bad things from coming into our lives, but He promises to be in them with us.

CHAPTER 12

The Conclusion to the Dream

I was trying to put my daughter under the law because I was afraid of the decisions she was making. I did not think she could make wise ones for herself, so I was determined to make them for her. I did not hear her; I only demanded from her, and she from me.

Would you like to know what the Lord used to start to transition her back to wholeness? What He used to make her feel as though living with us was a safe thing to do? Or better yet, what He used to show her who the real enemy was? The Lord was able to get a hold of my heart and to speak to me above the roar of the attacker, my fear, and other people's opinions. He told me to go to her and apologize for living in fear and reacting in a faithless way toward her.

We went for coffee and had a wonderful heart-to-heart conversation which started by me apologizing to her. After this conversation, the Lord started to change her heart toward us and toward the man she had been involved with.

The next piece of advice that I heard from the Spirit was to pray that God would send new friends for her to associate with. This happened at a birthday party we held for my oldest daughter. A friend who was an artist attended the party and immediately connected with my daughter. Over the next few months, she met other friends through this relationship. These new friends started questioning her unhealthy relationship with this individual. This led to a break in the hold that he had over her.

Next, the Lord spoke to my heart. After all the pain our family had gone through because of the enemy's efforts to destroy her, the

Lord showed me that I also had a part in it. I had lost my faith in the battle. I was making decisions not based on grace, faith, or patience. I was not truly trusting in the finished work of Jesus. I started out that way, but soon those fruits dropped.

But as I humbled myself before our great King, our Healer, what rose to the surface, that which was ripening in my spirit was love and gentleness and a newfound faith.

Again, once I heard the Spirit speak to my spirit. I was able to believe anew that God could and would not only protect her but would remove the enemy's influence that was surrounding her, causing her and me to react out of fear, anger, and frustration.

My fruits of love, peace, patience, kindness, goodness, and gentleness are still on the tree and growing in our relationship with each other because the Spirit within me is greater than the one in the world. And through the power of the Spirit and truth from God's Word, I am able to remain in the gap for these girls, praying without ceasing.

I have a strong relationship with each of them, and I am praying that they will see the love of God through my love for them and the words that I speak when they ask me about Jesus, the Bible, or my beliefs.

Colossians 1:11 (NIV) states, "Being strengthened with all power according to His glorious might so that you may have great endurance and patience." And in Romans 15:13 (NIV), we pray, "May the God of hope fill you with all joy and peace as you trust in Him, so that you may overflow with hope by the power of the Holy Spirit."

I have found that when I am in a season that seems as though I could be pointing a finger of judgment, because I have done that in the past, I have to remind myself that Jesus forgave me at the cross and put in me His Spirit. I have within me the same Spirit who is able to walk along with someone that seems to be off in their understanding of who God is and what Jesus has done. I am able to be gentle and at peace while I am loving them and finding joy in helping them.

Second Corinthians 6:1 states,

As God's co-workers we urge you not to receive God's grace in vain. For he says, "In the time of favor I heard you, and in the day of salvation I helped you." I tell you, now is the time of God's favor, now is the day of salvation.

2 Corinthians 6:1–2 (NIV)

We can keep our fruit, deciding not to give up on someone by reminding ourselves of what Jesus has done for us. We are His, and He purchased us with His precious blood. And we can remember how long it took us to get where we are. Second Corinthians 6:3–7 tells us how we prove that we are His servants sent to bring good news to those who the enemy is trying to destroy with his lies.

We put no stumbling block in anyone's path, so that our ministry will not be discredited. Rather, as servants of God we commend

ourselves in every way: in great endurance;

in troubles, hardships and distresses; in

beatings, imprisonments and riots; in hard

work, sleepless nights and hunger; in purity,

[we prove we are God's servants by our]

understanding, patience and kindness; in the

Holy Spirit and in sincere love; in truthful

speech and in the power of God; with

weapons of righteousness in the right hand

and in the left.

2 Corinthians 6:3–7 (NIV)

What Do God's Boundaries Look Like?

What do God's boundaries look like in our lives? Three things came to my mind after praying about this:

1.   God's justice and grace... These two aspects of God protect us from the wrath of God. We have mentioned several times that Jesus died on the cross, but we have not mentioned that He was satisfying the justice of God. When Adam was instructed not to eat of the tree that had on it the fruit of the knowledge of good and evil, he was told that if he did, the result would be death. This was a spiritual death that was passed down

to us. But we must confess that we are all accountable to God because of our own sinful thoughts and actions.

Jesus not only fulfilled the law of Moses, but He also became the payment for our sins, and in doing so, He satisfied God's demand for justice.

The Amplified Bible says it this way in Galatians 3:13,

Christ purchased our freedom and redeemed us from the curse of the Law and its condemnation by becoming a curse for us—for it is written, "CURSED IS EVERYONE WHO HANGS [crucified] ON A TREE (cross)"—

Galatians 3:13 (AMP)

A law tells you that you have to do something right now, whether you are able to or not. The law points out your sin when you break it, but it does not show mercy. If you do not keep the whole law, then there is a punishment.

Thankfully, we who are in Christ are given His grace. Grace is the unconditional love of God bestowed on you. "For by grace are ye saved through faith; and that not of yourselves: it is the gift of God: Not of works, lest any man should boast" (Ephesians 2:8–9, KJV).

2.   The Word of God... Jesus used the Word of God to counter the temptations that the enemy was throwing at Him. Matthew 4:1–11 tells us that Jesus was led by the Spirit into the wilderness. He was alone; He was fasting for forty days, so He was hungry and weak physically, and the enemy was twisting the Word to try to confuse Jesus. But Jesus' use of the Word to fight the enemy kept Him from being defeated and enabled Him to fulfill His mission here on earth. His protection was not in His ability to argue; it was in the authority of God's Word.

Do you realize that Jesus set boundaries for Himself so that we could be saved? If He did not use the Word and stay in submission to God's authority, believing it was true and resulting in the fulfillment of the promises God had given Him, we would never have the opportunity for salvation. Have you ever done this? Do you quote scripture to the enemy when he attacks your thoughts? If not, then you should start! We fight our battles in submission to God's will. We do this by believing in our hearts then speaking the Word aloud and with authority.

God has given us His Word to set boundaries for our life also.

Second Timothy 3:16–17 states,

All scripture is inspired by God, and can profitably be used for teaching, for refuting error, for guiding people's lives and teaching them to be holy. This is how the man that is dedicated to God becomes fully equipped and ready for any good work.

2 Timothy 3:16–17 (TJB)

3.   His Spirit... The Spirit prays for us and protects us from being deceived.

In the same way, the Spirit helps us in our weakness. We do not know what we ought to pray for, but the Spirit himself intercedes for us through wordless groans. And he who searches our hearts knows the mind of the Spirit, because the Spirit intercedes for God's people in accordance with the will of God.

Romans 8:26–27 (NIV)

Also, we are sealed with the Spirit; He is our boundary, protecting us.

In Him you also trusted, after you heard the word of truth, the gospel of your salvation; in whom also, having believed, you were sealed with the Holy Spirit of promise, who is the guarantee of our inheritance until the redemption of the purchased possession, to the praise of His glory.

Ephesians 1:13–14 (NKJV)

Ephesians 1:13–14 (NKJV) Not every spirit that speaks is the Holy Spirit. Therefore, we are told to test the spirits to see if they are from God.

Beloved, believe not every spirit, but try the spirits whether they are of God: because many false prophets are gone out into the world.

Hereby know ye the Spirit of God: Every spirit that confesseth that Jesus Christ is come in the flesh is of God.

And every spirit that confesseth not that Jesus Christ is come in the flesh is not of God: and this is the spirit of antichrist, whereof ye have heard that it should come, and even now already is it in the world.

Ye are of God, little children, and have overcome them: because greater is he that is in you, than he that is in the world.

1 John 4:1–4 (KJV)

Chapter 13

The Unseen Enemy

Have you ever listened to a preacher or read a sign in front of a church and said to yourself, "That's not what the Bible says"? We have whole groups of people that are destroyed by their lack of knowledge. There was a time when I just believed anything that was told to me like so many others, but it kept me trapped in guilt, condemnation, and sinful behaviors.

I believe that people take scripture out of context when they do not explore what other passages speak on concerning the same subject or when they only read half of what is being said. For instance, I was not taught how or why I should have a thankful heart when I am praying.

Now I realize that it may sound silly to have a thankful heart when things are not going well, but according to Philippians 4:6–7 (NKJV), we are told to pray with thanksgiving. It says,

Be anxious for nothing, but in everything by prayer and supplication, with thanksgiving, let your requests be made known to God, and the peace of God, which surpasses all understanding, will guard your hearts and minds through Christ Jesus.

Philippians 4:6–7 (NKJV)

I have come to understand that I can trust God in all things; therefore, I can have a thankful heart knowing that He loves me, has a good plan for me, can meet my every need, and is able to give me the strength to go through all things.

We are also told in scripture that without faith, it is impossible to please God. "But without faith it is impossible to please him: for he that cometh to God must believe that he is, and that he is a rewarder of them that diligently seek him" (Hebrews 11:6, KJV).

These verses do not say that everything will turn out the way I want them to, but it does say that in giving thanks to God, it shows that I am trusting that He knows what is best for me. And that He will guard or protect my heart and mind. He does this by giving me the perspective I need throughout the process of being conformed to Christ in any given situation.

The verses also do not say that we will not have emotions or feel pain because we certainly do. The problem comes in when we let the emotion overrule the truth of God's word. For many years I allowed my emotions and the situations around me to dictate what God was doing or not doing in my heart, mind, and life. I let the word of God have the second place, so when there was a difficult situation, I was not really trusting God.

I spent so much time crying over my problems and begging God to help me. Or even worse, asking someone else to step into the place that only God can or should be in. I thought that was being humble. But it was not humility; humility is knowing that you cannot do something of yourself, but the one you have gone to is able to help you or supply your need. When we pray with thanksgiving, we are showing that we believe Jesus is who He says He is and will do what He promises to do as the Holy Spirit reveals those truths to our hearts.

Another truth that goes along with thanksgiving is we should know that our difficulties are the instrument that can be used to draw us to God and allow us to see His power, provision, love, mercy, and any other attribute He wishes to reveal about Himself to us.

God has an individual path that He wants to lead us on, and He tells us clearly that the road will be paved with difficulties, but we are to be of good cheer because He has overcome the world. "These things I have spoken unto you, that in me you might have peace. In the world ye shall have tribulation: but be of good cheer; I have overcome the world" (John 16:33, KJV).

The unseen enemy is those thoughts that tell you that you have a right and expectation to be upset, guilty, anxious, or angry when things are not going your way. But those are lies that take you away from God's peace and lead you into the net of confusion, weakness, mistrust, faithlessness, and sin.

Hosea 4:6 tells us,

My people are destroyed for lack of knowledge: because thou has rejected knowledge, I will also reject thee, thou shalt be no priest to me: seeing thou hast forgotten the law of thy God, I will also forget thy children.

Hosea 4:6 (KJV)

Paul very clearly teaches us truths that we need to digest and let sink into our hearts, spirits, and souls.

For this reason, since the day we heard about you, we have not stopped praying for you. We continually ask God to fill you with the knowledge of His will through all the wisdom and understanding that the Spirit gives, so that you may live a life worthy of the Lord and please Him in every way; bearing fruit in every good work, growing in the knowledge of God, being strengthened with all power according to His glorious might so that you may have great endurance and patience, and giving joyful thanks to the Father who has qualified you to share in the inheritance of his holy people in the kingdom of light. For He has rescued us from the dominion of darkness and brought us into the kingdom of the Son he loves, in whom we have redemption, the forgiveness of sins.

Colossians 1:9–14 (NIV)

What a wonderful truth Paul is sharing with us; he is praying that we would come to understand everything that we have as a result of being the children of God. That we would realize what the Spirit of God wants us to have and is willing to give to us so that we may have power, endurance, patience, joy with a thankful heart, and bear fruit in every good work. I believe he also wants to make sure we understand that we have been rescued from the dominion of darkness (sin and lack of knowledge of God); therefore, they do not have to dominate our lives.

God considers us holy people who live in the kingdom of light by the power of His Son. And in Jesus, we have redemption (the action of saving or being saved from sin, error, or evil... the action of regaining a possession of something in exchange for payment or clearing a debt). Jesus paid our sin debt with His blood on the cross.

In Colossians, chapter 2, Paul tells his readers to live according to the true faith in Christ, not according to false teaching. Verses 6 to 8 in the Jerusalem Bible state,

You must live your whole life according to the Christ you have received—Jesus the Lord; you must be rooted in Him, built on Him, and held firm by the faith you have been taught, and full of thanksgiving. Make sure that no one traps you and deprives you of your freedom some second hand, empty, rational philosophy based on the principles of this world instead of on Christ.

Colossians 2:6–8 (TJB)

God takes His truth very seriously. And He expects us to cherish what Jesus has done for us and what the Holy Spirit provides for us. And if we do not, this next scripture is a warning of judgment to those who teach false doctrines, attack His church, and destroy His people.

Revelation 19:15 states,

Now out of His mouth goes a sharp sword, that with it He should strike the nations. And He Himself will rule them with a rod of iron. He Himself treads the winepress of the fierceness and wrath of Almighty God.

Revelation 19:15 (NKJV)

As we discussed earlier in the book, faith comes by hearing. But it is not enough to hear just anything that comes off of the top of a preacher's head. If the preacher is representing the Word of God, then the preacher has to have wisdom in preaching. We can learn something from studying a book or listening to someone speak on a subject, but wisdom is more than just head knowledge; wisdom requires experience and our respect of God, His Word, and His Spirit.

To know wisdom and instruction; to perceive the words of understanding; To receive the instruction of wisdom, justice, and judgment, and equity;

176

To give subtilty to the simple, to the young man knowledge and discretion.

A wise man will hear and will increase learning; and a man of understanding shall attain unto wise counsels:

To understand a proverb, and the interpretation; the words of the wise, and their dark sayings.

The fear of the LORD is the beginning of knowledge: but fools despise wisdom and instruction.

Proverbs 1:2–7 (KJV)

When the enemy is at work, he will twist God's Word; he will cause you to question God's Word; he will cause you to question God's names, attributes, and power. He will try to make you believe that God's Word is unreliable. The enemy is subtle, and at times, especially when you are unaware, he is masterful at deception. He makes you believe that the sin that has a stronghold on you is impossible to break. He makes it easy for us to excuse behaviors that are damaging our lives and those around us. He causes us to look at others instead of examining our own hearts. Most of all, he gets us to believe the lies instead of searching for the truth. It is easy to follow the enemy with his friends who are called the flesh and the world.

Ephesians 6:12 states,

For our struggle is not against flesh and blood, but against the rulers, against the authorities, against the powers of this dark world and against the spiritual forces of evil in the heavenly realms.

Ephesians 6:12 (NIV)

Thank God that He has equipped us with all of the resources that we need to keep our fruit from being devoured! Ephesians 6:13 (AMP) tells us to put on the armor of God.

Therefore, put on the complete armor of God, so that you will be able to [successfully] resist and stand your ground in the evil day [of danger], and having done everything [that the crisis demands], to stand firm [in your place, fully prepared, immovable, victorious].

Ephesians 6:13 (AMP)

When we put on the whole armor of God, we will not be deceived through bad or unbiblical doctrine. There are many enemies to the gospel, and the most dangerous is the twisting of the Word. If we look at the serpent in the garden, we will see that a twist of one or two words caused doubt. God told Adam not to eat of the tree, but the enemy asked the woman, "Did God really say you were not to eat from any of the trees in the garden?" (Genesis 3:1b, NLT) Notice, the serpent did not go directly to Adam. Why? Maybe because Adam had clearly been given the truth directly from God. And maybe because he knew Eve had secondhand information and thought she could be more easily tempted. So again, make sure you know what the Lord has spoken to you, and to the best of your ability, compare scripture with scripture to discover the truth.

We may not do everything perfectly as we enter a new season of life. We may feel as though we are being attacked and do not know how to respond. We may even respond badly and sin or cause others to sin. Or we may feel as though our fruit is being stolen from us. In these situations, we may feel like a failure, but by the grace of God and the finished work of Jesus, and the continuing prompting of the Holy Spirit, the tree will produce more fruit in the future.

And yet, now we read in the book of John, Jesus is the True Vine, and we are the branches. Jesus also said,

Abide in Me, and I in you. As the branch cannot bear fruit of itself, unless it abides in the vine [or in our illustration, on the tree], neither can you, unless you abide in Me.

John 15:4 (NKJV)

CHAPTER 14

A Healthy Tree Needs to Be Pruned

Now there is one last step that is vital to proper growth and production: it is the process of pruning. When is the proper time to prune an apple tree? The answer might surprise you; it is in the dead of winter when everything seems dead and dormant. When nature has gone to sleep and all is at rest.

Did you know that a good winter freeze can prevent some insects that might harm the tree in other seasons from developing? The winter freeze also helps to promote soil stabilization.

Do you know what and why we prune? Pruning is when you take off the dead branches on the tree that are no longer of any value to the tree's growth or production. We all have things in our lives that are no longer producing anything of value.

It is like when it is time to clean out the closet, but you do not want to throw out your favorite dress. You know it is old and no longer fits, but you felt so beautiful in it, and the memories are so precious, that you just stick it back in the closet with hopes that maybe, someday, it will fit, and you would have the opportunity to wear it again. It might be hidden, but you know it is there. Every once in a while, you pull it out and try it on. You know you cannot wear it anywhere, and you feel disappointed when you cannot zip up the zipper, but the feelings overwhelm your decision to part with it.

Then your daughter comes over to your house to help you organize; she takes out the dress, looks at it, looks at you, and immediately puts it in the goodwill bag. You may protest, but deep down inside, you know you are not losing anything; and now, you have room for something new, and it might be more valuable to let someone else have the opportunity to wear it.

We all have "favorites" in our life. What is it in your life that you know you should let go of and move beyond? Is it a relationship, a dream, an interest, or a ministry? Do not be discouraged if God takes it away. He knows what is best for you. He is doing a new thing, and it will bring life and joy to your soul, as well as fit into your new life.

Spindly Branches...

The Gardener also wants to cut off the spindly branches that are growing out of the center of the tree. These branches are cut off so that there is an open center to the tree so that the tree can have lots of air circulation. These are the things that are crowding your life and mind. They are usually sticking straight up, so you cannot help but notice them. These branches represent the energy we waste when we spend time worrying about needless tasks or about things that we have no control over. When we let these pressures crowd our minds instead of meditating on the Word of God, we waste our time and energy. We are told to fix our eyes on Jesus. When we do, we are letting the fresh breeze of the Spirit surround us and bring in new thoughts and ideas to our hearts and minds.

There have been many times in my life when the circumstances have not changed, but my perspective has. I have noticed that when I allow the Word of God to take the place of worry or stress or anger, I am then able to sense His presence and feel His gentle touch as He encircles and engulfs me with His sweet fragrance of love. He replaces my fear with faith, my worry with song, my distraction with hope, and my anger with grace.

Pruning Is Beneficial

There is another interesting lesson to this pruning. There should be enough room not only for the air circulation but also for birds to be able to fly through. What do birds represent? Freedom. They can walk on the earth, fly in the sky, and swim in the water. They move about freely. Also, they can get food from the ground (worms, seeds, fruits, and berries), food from the oceans and seas (fish and sea creatures), and they can find food in the skies (insects). When we make space for God, we experience *freedom*! Do you realize that the Holy Spirit is represented by a Dove? And when He has space to move around in our lives, He enables us to live in freedom!

The last reason for pruning that I will mention really had an impact on me. The Gardener who wants lots of fruit production must cut off one-third of the previous year's growth. He also must cut off overcrowded apple spurs and shorten long extended stems.

An apple spur is where the fruit is grown on the tree. On my tree, the fruit grows on the small thorn-shaped branches that extend off of a main tree branch.

We own an apple tree, and my husband prunes it yearly, but we did not know about apple spurs. So not knowing, we never cut them off. We thought the more, the better. We found out the hard way that this is not true!

We had a season of plenty. Our tree was packed with large, almost ripe Granny Smith apples. There were so many we did not even care if the squirrels helped themselves to a few. But then, one day, while we were working in the yard, we heard this loud crack. We had heard this crack before when one of our damaged trees had split, but we had never seen a good, healthy tree split.

We immediately tried to save it from completely coming away from the trunk. I ran inside, opened my computer, and started searching for the answer as to how to save our tree. I did not want to lose the fruit that we had been waiting for so long to harvest. As I read different articles, I found that you can brace the branch up and screw it back to the trunk, and it might heal. But just as I was running back to tell my husband, I heard that dying cry from the tree. It had cracked again and had broken off and was resting on a lower smaller limb.

My heart sank. I was overwhelmed with sadness. I really could not understand how this happened. I thought we had been doing everything right and that we had finally had our harvest come in. Now, I felt robbed and confused. But that was not the end of it. Because of the weight of the first branch falling, it caused the weaker, smaller branch that was just below the broken branch to crack, and a short time later, we lost that one also.

My beautiful, mature, well-endowed tree had just lost two of what I thought were strong, well-developed branches. Boy, do I wish that I had understood that the abundance of fruit did not mean that all was well for that season. The tree was not ready to carry all that weight.

What I realized later that season was that even though I would have liked to have the full crop, we still had quite a few apples that year. The truth is, it is still producing fruit, even in its awkward, broken state.

Carrying Too Heavy a Load

So, what does this look like in our lives? Two examples come to my mind. The first would be the larger branch. There was a time when I was being used in many capacities at our church, and God was growing me in many areas. I saw fruit being produced, but I was carrying a heavy load.

So, everyone around me kept looking at the fruit and thinking that all was good. I was loving, gentle, kind, easy to have a good relationship with, but I was full of pain. My fruit looked good on the outside, and my branch looked sturdy, but amongst the good was something that was not healthy. I felt overwhelmed and knew inside that something was wrong with my heart.

I had just come through a major spiritual battle and had not taken the time to be healed completely. And just like my tree, once the split started happening, and we did not know enough to prop it up, I had been separating myself from the tree (the True Vine, Jesus), looking for man's approval rather than believing that I was indeed being taken care of by Jesus and that what He had been producing in me was good. I remember saying constantly during the three-year battle that I had been going through serving under a new leader, "I feel so insecure." I had constantly been told that I was not good enough and that I was not capable of meeting this person's expectations. I had been deeply hurt, and all those feelings of helplessness as a child and young adult found their way back to my heart.

Isn't it true in the Christian life that we want to produce a harvest of good fruit? I believe the answer is yes. But I am slowly learning that just like everything else in God's kingdom, there is a time to eat, a time to sleep, a time to go to battle, and a time to rest from war and be healed. I should have stopped and asked for help, but instead, I kept going and felt the tension and the strain until I was almost at my breaking point.

But unlike us, the True Vinedresser knows how to prune the tree, to cut off what is weighing us down. I did not know how to stop meeting other people's expectations or recognize the emotional stress that went along with not saying "no." I wanted their approval. I put too much emphasis on myself and not on Jesus' acceptance of me. The enemy kept reminding me, or better yet, accusing me of not being enough, so I kept doing. And I was believing his lies and repeating them to myself aloud.

I remember hearing the Lord say to me several times, "Stop saying that you are insecure." Jesus knew who I was and the fruit He was developing in me, but at the time, I did not recognize it; I just felt the cracking of the branches as I was being weighed down. We are told to keep our eyes fixed on Jesus because we cannot do anything apart from Christ. I was being weighed down. I was trying to focus on the Son, but I let the need for approval have my attention, so my heart kept breaking.

The truth is that we are never enough by ourselves, but through Christ, we are more than conquerors. Jesus kept wrapping His loving arms around me and holding me, so unlike my tree, I did not break. I did not have to be thrown away or burnt. Thank God! But the Lord knew I needed to rest and to be healed, so in a gentle and quiet voice, He told me to come away and rest in Him. Which I obediently did.

Jesus is the One who heals the brokenhearted, but when we do not take the time to be healed and be fastened securely back to the tree, or when we overcrowd the branch and think it is all about ourselves and how we look in the kingdom, that is when we need to ask God if we need His pruning or an extra measure of His wisdom. The Dove cannot come through a crowded bunch of branches pushing their own way to heaven. Likewise, a broken, heavy-laden branch will not stay on the tree without extra support.

Chapter 15

Leading Up to the Battle

The second pruning in my life came when my husband went into the hospital. My husband's illnesses stopped me in my tracks. This particular episode happened on the very night that some of my obligations had ended for our Christmas break. On my way home from our Bible study, I had heard a voice in my spirit say, "Tonight, I will take your husband." This was not the gentle, loving voice of my Savior; it was the enemy, and I recognized it at once. To my amazement, my immediate response was, "Oh no, you won't."

This response was due to another dream that I had had. It took place prior to my husband's hospitalization and after an unexpected, answered prayer had taken place one Saturday afternoon.

My husband had been getting weaker and weaker from his illness. One day we were in the kitchen, where a light had blown out in the ceiling fixture. He could not walk across the room to fix the light. He wanted to use a stepladder, the ones we keep in the kitchen so the grandchildren can help bake a delicious snack, but he could not carry it across the room. He was so upset with his own weakness and inability to do such a simple task that he told me to leave. He did not want me to see him this way.

I went upstairs and just fell on the floor and cried out to God. I was a heaping pile of sorrow and pain. I hated to see the love of my life dying before my very eyes, and I hated the thought of losing him. While I was crying out to God and asking Him if He was going to take my husband home, I heard in my spirit those familiar words, "Get up and worship Me." So, I did; I got up, went into our bathroom, and started cleaning. I always seem to clean when something is bothering me.

I washed down every wall with bleach; I washed the floor and every fixture in the room. I scrubbed the tub, toilet, and sink. That room was shining, and I was singing and praising God the entire time. Then when I was about to finish cleaning, I heard a voice from the bottom of the stairs. It was my husband yelling up to me, asking me what I was doing. His voice was clear and loud; it had power again. He did not sound weak or out of breath. I told him what I was doing and asked him what he was doing. His response filled me with an unspeakable joy. He told me how he replaced the light bulb, did some yard work with my son, and then cleaned the kitchen. This gave me a hope that he would not be taken from me at this time. But the enemy was not done with his attacks. Next came the dream that sent me to the throne of God for wisdom and understanding.

Unshakable Dream

In my dream, I was driving home from my Tuesday night Bible study, and it was dark and rainy. As I came toward the center of my town, I noticed that there was no one on the road, even though it was lined with stores, coffee shops, and restaurants that normally would have people coming and going from them.

It was eerily quiet, and I had the sense that something was wrong. As I slowly drove along the main street, I saw men on the sidewalks and walking through the streets with guns. They seemed to be watching for something or someone. As I continued to drive, I noticed that they were looking intently at my car as I passed by them. Some were pointing at me, and I sensed that some of the men were even talking about me, but they seemed to let me pass without any resistance.

I could feel fear and apprehension building inside of me, and I was asking myself, "Where is everyone, and what is going on?" As

188

I left the center of town and headed down the main street that was connected to my street, I was instantly aware that they had been watching me.

The street was lined on both sides for as far as I could see, with men pointing machine guns at me. As I passed them, they started firing at me from all sides. I just put my head down and started driving as fast as I could.

Then terror filled my soul. I was afraid to go home. I was filled with the thought that my husband was dead and that there was no one to go home to. At that moment, I awoke from my dream. I still had the feeling of fear; it felt as though I had really just lived through this horrible scene.

Understanding the Dream

I spent several days talking to the Lord, asking Him what the dream meant. I had already released my husband and his health to the Lord and had asked for wisdom going forward. My husband had stage 4 emphysema and had been experiencing several flare-ups the past year. I was also aware that he had congestive heart failure, even though it had not been diagnosed.

My dad had also had congestive heart failure, and I watched him die a few years earlier. I saw my husband show the same symptoms. So, I thought the dream was about my husband being killed. I did not know if this was God's way of telling me to let go of my husband because it was his time. So, I went to the Word of God and asked the Holy Spirit to reveal God's will to me in this situation. He led me to several verses. These are a few of them:

"Many are the afflictions of the righteous, but the LORD delivers him out of them all" (Psalm 34:19, NKJV).

I have seen his ways, and will heal him; I will also lead him,
And restore comforts to him And to his mourners.
"I create the fruit of the lips:
Peace, peace to him who is far off and to him who is near,"
Says the LORD, "And I will heal him."
Isaiah 57:18–19 (NKJV)

"Come, and let us return to the LORD; For he has torn, but He
will heal us; He has stricken, but He will bind up"
(Hosea 6:1, NKJV).

"He shall call upon Me, and I will answer him; I will be with
him in trouble and will deliver him and honor him. With long life I
will satisfy him, and show him My salvation"
(Psalm 91:15–16, NKJV).

"But He was wounded for our transgressions, He was bruised
for our iniquities; The chastisement for our peace was upon Him; And
by His stripes we are healed"
(Isaiah 53:5, NKJV).

"God is not a man, that He should lie, Nor a son of man, that
He should repent. He has said, and will He not do? Or has He spoken,
and will He not make it good?"
(Numbers 23:19, NKJV)

I now had an assurance that my husband was not going to die. When I prayed and asked the Lord if my husband had died in the dream, the answer to my question came in another question. The question that I was asked was, "What kept me from going home?" My answer as I thought about it was, I had assumed that my husband had died or had been killed, and I was too afraid to go home. I had believed the worse possible outcome. After thinking about the question, I realized I woke up before I got to my house; I really did not know if he was at the house or if he was dead. My fear left me with the assumption that he was dead.

Then the Lord showed me that the enemy was trying to kill both of us. He had been throwing everything he could at us. And yet, he had not been able to kill me spiritually, and he would not be able to physically take my husband either. I was suddenly aware of all the ways that the enemy had tried to stop me from going to church and had even tried to keep me from ministry, yet he was not able to complete his goal. Now we were about to see how the enemy was going to try to take my husband's life.

The Battle Had Begun

It was December 9th. I had just finished an exceptionally long day at the church. It was our last Bible study before the Christmas break. My team and I had organized, set up, and cleaned up a brunch for over two hundred women. I had gone home for a few hours but then returned to pick up the food that was being catered as well as set up and clean up the dinner for our evening study of about eighty women. During the evening study, I had given my testimony and had a meal with my group. I was exhausted from the day and the events that I had set up.

As I drove home a little later than usual, I heard those words, "Tonight, I will take your husband." I was driving on the same road and in the same location as in my dream. I was also aware that it was very dark and that it was raining. The attack from the enemy was about to take place, but I did not know how it would play out. But as I said earlier, my answer to that voice was not fear-based. It was confidence in what the Lord had been revealing to me. And confidence in the scriptures that He had given to me, as His promises of protection and deliverance.

By the time I returned home, my husband was in bed. He asked me how my day went and then fell back to sleep. I also went to sleep.

A few hours later, my husband woke up not being able to breathe. We gave him all the medication that his doctor had prescribed, but it did nothing for his breathing. He insisted that I call an ambulance. This was the first time we had ever called one.

The ambulance arrived along with paramedics, they wanted him to lay on the gurney, but he refused. This aggravated the medical team because they needed to get him down a flight of stairs. After walking down, the stairs with the medical team's assistance, he was rushed to the hospital. My husband could not lay on the gurney even in the ambulance, which made the ambulance drivers terribly upset. He could not and would not lay down at the hospital. They had to do all his tests with him standing up.

Everyone was looking at his lungs. What they found through days of testing and blood work was that he was having systolic heart failure, congestive heart failure, pneumonia, and a flare-up of emphysema, all while holding twenty-one pounds of fluid. The doctors also believed that there must be blocked arteries and that he might need triple bypass surgery.

We spent the next eleven days in two different hospitals, in intensive care units. My husband sat in a bed for most of those days. We were later told that if he had laid down while the fluid was in him, he would have died. We were also told that both his lung and heart were at 20 percent. Prior to this episode, the doctors were talking to my husband about lung replacement. This was no longer an option. Now they were just trying to keep him alive.

I had spent eleven days before the throne of God, worshipping, praising, and interceding for my husband's life. I had some trusted sisters in Christ whom I had sent the verses and asked to stand in faith with me. I know this was a big ask because in my church, we did not see many healings, and I had not heard of any miracles. We always heard of how faithful people were during their sickness and how they had ministered to those around them. What I was asking of them was radical to our thinking.

But during that time, I did not care what anyone thought of me—my belief in healing or my walk with God. I was going into battle for my husband's life, and I knew he would come out alive! I was standing on the Word of God. I had so much belief and faith in what the Spirit had told me through the scripture that I even told my friends that if they could not stand in faith with me, then they should get out of my circle and not pray at all. My first branch of wanting people's approval or caring about their opinion of my spiritual walk had been cut down.

Meanwhile, we were getting ready for Christmas. Our family was using Facetime so my husband could watch the grandchildren decorate our Christmas tree that they had bought for us. I was spending time in the ICU as my children quietly prayed that they would not be saying goodbye to their dad for the last time. I was comforting and reassuring grandchildren who needed to know that we serve a great God who hears our prayers, speaks truth to us, and responds to our every need. Meanwhile, as I noted above, I was sending out emails of verses and promises asking people to stand in agreement with what the Spirit was leading me to pray. As well as speaking with doctors and nurses and trying to understand the complexity of his illnesses and what the next steps were.

The doctors were telling us that Chip would be fully disabled and would not be working any longer. They also said he would have to sleep downstairs, which meant moving our bedroom and rearranging our house, including putting a shower in downstairs bathroom. We were also told that he would need to sleep in an incline position, so we should purchase a new bed with the mechanics to do so. And we would need medical equipment for his breathing at night.

But thankfully, I was ready for this hospitalization time. God had prepared me for this battle. I had been spending a great deal of time studying about healing, bending my knee to God's will, and watching God work through prayer. Now we (Holy Spirit, Jesus, and I) were in constant communion going before our Heavenly Father for His mercy and life-giving power. As well as reminding Him and myself of the finished work of Christ on the cross and that by His stripes, we are healed.

It was a challenging time: I had to watch my words, guard my heart, rely on the Word alone, put up walls of protection against thoughts and feeling that others wanted to share with me during this experience. I even had to correct people's words in connection to what was happening. But God had given me the strength and protection we needed to get through. My husband did not die that night, nor did he need triple bypass surgery, nor did we change our room around or purchase a new bed or medical equipment, and my husband went back to work right after the holidays.

And as many of you who have fought the good fight of faith at various times in your life know, once you think the battle is over, you let down your guard.

A short while after my husband came home, we were able to celebrate Christmas together as a family at my house. We rejoiced in God's mercy and loving-kindness toward us because we knew that the enemy had come to steal, rob, and destroy our lives. But instead, we both, my husband and I, felt as though God had given us our lives back.

But It Was Not Over Yet...

Scripture tells us that the enemy comes to rob us, and you never know when he is coming. I had let my defenses down because I thought the battle was over. But a few days after my husband came home from the hospital, he had a flare-up of his lungs. This really set me back. I did not expect or understand what was happening. People in my church were amazed that he was home and that he had come through this ordeal so quickly. He was even in church the day after he came home from the hospital. He was walking around and living like a new man.

I had not been taught anything from my church of how healing comes about. Everything that I did know came from a few television programs and the understanding of what the Spirit was revealing to me through these ministries.

I had had the experience of laying my hands on my grandchildren. And when I had laid my hands on my grandchildren, they were usually healed either immediately or within a day or two. I was expecting the same for my husband, a complete healing without any setbacks. But that is not what I was seeing with my physical eyes. So again, I went to the Lord and asked what was going on. The answer was simple and clear: it would be a progressive healing. We both had a lot to learn.

What I found over the next few months was that there was so

much guilt and condemnation in my husband that he believed that he could not be healed and that he was getting what he deserved.

I also had come to realize that when that flare-up occurred, I stumbled in my faith. I let the enemy rob me of the miracle that had taken place. I was ashamed to say that he was healed just in case people found out that he had a flare-up and he was on medication now for his heart.

What I did not know was that this is a normal tactic of the enemy. I did not know how to resist him until two years later. It took two years for me to realize that it is not a magical formula that heals people; it is not repeating verses for the sake of repeating verses, nor is it by our own power or desire; it is the will of God as the Spirit makes alive in you His truth. It is knowing Jesus and believing He has a plan, a will, and a destiny for each of us.

The Lord has shown me that I had faith the day I prayed while upstairs cleaning my bathroom. That is when I believed God and showed it by getting up and worshipping Him. That is when my prayer was being answered, and it was manifested during the hospital stays. My husband, who could not walk a few steps prior to his hospitalization, left the hospital and returned to work.

After my husband's hospitalization and returning to work, the Lord told me to come aside, author this book, and get healed myself.

CHAPTER 16

I Have Since Learned a Few Things About Healing For God's Children

> Whether it is emotional, physical, relational, or spiritual healing, it starts with God and ends with God! He is the One who gives us the promises and speaks to our hearts.

> Jesus, while on earth, healed people before He went to the cross.

> Jesus healed those who had faith and came to Him asking for it.

> Jesus healed anyone who asked and truly believed He could and He would. There were even times when the sick person was not present, but the one asking was the one who believed.

> Jesus healed those who were persistent in expecting Him to be gracious and heal their loved ones, even when they were not of Jewish descent.

> Jesus also healed those who believed He had the power to heal them but were afraid to publicly come forth. They received it through touching Him.

> Jesus healed people even when they did not know who He was.

> Jesus explained some of His reasons for healing, and others He did not.

> Sometimes Jesus heals us even when we do not know how to ask for it or that we have been looking for it until He opens our eyes.

➤ Jesus instructed some people to be obedient to an instruction that would show their faith so the miracle would take place.

➤ Some people showed their faith by bringing their friends to Jesus.

➤ Healing does not come by a magic formula, and it is not in reciting verses repeatedly, as though we are able to make something happen by our own capacity; healing comes through faith in believing that it is part of our salvation.

➤ Jesus asked some people if they wanted to be healed before He healed them.

➤ *We must be careful as Christians that we do not get caught up in one way of healing or that there has to be a set of rules or practices in order for healing to take place. We also will have an easier time asking and believing that God will answer our prayers and direct us in the healing process if we understand and think on the following truths about Jesus.*

➤ God loves us fully and unconditionally.

➤ We, as Christians, get caught up in our beliefs and think we cannot be healed because of sin in our lives. We need to know that God has forgiven us of all sin, past, present, and future, once we confess them and ask for His forgiveness. He is not looking at our sins but is looking at us through the righteousness of Jesus. And because of the work on the cross and our faith in what Jesus has done for us, we are no longer under the curse of the law.

➤ God does not put sickness on us.

➤ God sees us in Jesus and not apart from Him. Through His name, we can speak to our mountains to be removed. This happens when we really see who Jesus is as our Savior, Redeemer, and Curse Breaker...

➤ By Jesus' stripes, we are healed.

➤ We must accept His forgiveness and then use the authority that He has given us to further His kingdom.

➤ Jesus has already healed us or provided for the promise He wants to give us. Once we believe that it is part of our salvation, and His Spirit is speaking to us personally, then speak it out with praise and thanksgiving. This belief is from the heart, not the head. Knowing something intellectually is different from a Spirit-to-spirit revelation.

➤ We need to stand on the firm foundation that "God is not a respecter of persons," meaning that God provides everyone an opportunity to be healed or blessed through the salvation Jesus has provided. Our part is to believe what Jesus has accomplished on the cross for us and to claim it for ourselves as we are led by the Spirit.

➤ We must also believe that God is not a liar. He is always faithful and true to His promises. If He has said it, He will do it, and if He has done it, He will manifest it. But the manifestation of any promise is according to our believing.

➤ And most importantly, we must see that whether it be emotional, physical, or spiritual healing, it is for God's glory, and it exalts Jesus.

Right about now, you may be saying those are nice truths, but what do they have to do with healing or with any of God's promises being manifested in our lives? The Scriptures tell us how God's promises are manifested in the natural realm coming from the spiritual realm. Why don't we look at some of the components to a manifestation of God's working in our lives?

The Amplified Bible says it this way,

Christ has purchased our freedom and redeemed us from the curse of the Law and its condemnation by becoming a curse for us—for it is written, "CURSED IS EVERYONE WHO HANGS [crucified] ON A TREE (cross)"—

Galatians 3:13 (AMP)

Jesus has already broken the curse of the Law; we are no longer subject to it, and therefore, we can expect healing if the Spirit of God has given us that promise.

I do believe that Jesus has an individual path for each of us. When we read in Hebrews, chapter 11, we see those whose faith caused them to do right by God, there are those that did not see death, there were those who were saved from destruction, those who received the inheritance and were able to bear children by the power of God.

But then there were others who died in faith, not receiving the promises but seeing them afar off.

We have to know what the Spirit of God is saying to us personally. Do you see the foundation of truth that has to be laid? I am not saying that every person needs to know every one of the above truths, but I do believe when we do not have a firm foundation of what Jesus has done for us and where the power actually comes from, then the enemy is able to rob us of the truth that God wants us to have so that faith can be activated.

As I mentioned before, grace is God's part. God showed His love toward us while we were still sinners by sending Jesus to die for those sins (Roman 5:8). Jesus provided everything that we needed when He suffered and died for us. Then He went to the grave and conquered it. He broke the curse that was holding us captive and set us free to live the life that He had ordained us to have.

Relational and Spiritual Healing

Do you remember that after Adam and Eve sinned, death entered the world, and with it came the curse? Jesus paid for that sin and broke the ability of the curse that made us subject to it.

Do you realize that the first law that was broken was when Adam and Eve disobeyed God in the Garden of Eden? He told them not to eat of the tree of the knowledge of good and evil or else they would die. But they believed another voice instead of God's.

And do you also remember what God did in response to their sin? He went looking for them. He, God Himself, sacrificed an innocent animal on their behalf. He then took the blood-laden skins and covered their guilt and shame. Jesus is the sacrifice whose blood was shed on our behalf. His blood did more than cover our sins; it washed them away. It removed them forever. God remembers our sin no more once we put our faith in what Jesus did for us.

Adam and Eve had to leave the garden so that they would not eat of the tree of life and live forever in their sin. God at that time promised the Seed, which would crush the head of the serpent, our enemy. That Seed (Jesus) gave us an invitation into the life (the Promised Land) that God had intended for us to live in. And when we accept that invitation (belief in the Lord Jesus Christ), we are seated in heavenly places. In other words, we get to see into the spiritual world and hear the voice of God speak to us personally.

Jesus is the promised Seed who crushed the head of the serpent and released those who were waiting for the promised One, who would do the work that God had ordained by His words. We have been released from the power of darkness; we have freedom to make choices that line up with God's will and purposes.

Then Jesus rose again to heaven, where the Father accepted His blood sacrifice on our behalf. Our punishment was paid for by Jesus' death and His sacrifice. It occurred to me the other day that some people still think that God is mad at them. So, if He is mad, then would not that mean that Jesus also is mad.

Is God Mad at Me Still?

Think about this for a moment: Jesus is the one who left heaven and gave up everything to take on flesh. Jesus is the one who was mocked and ridiculed. Jesus is the one who was rejected by His friends and His religious leaders and sold by one of His disciples. He was stripped, punched, beaten, had a crown of thorns placed on His head, whipped, and then hung on a cross. In my book, that is not how anyone would want to be treated and could make anyone hold a grudge.

And yet, some of His last few words were: **"Father forgive them for they know not what they do"** (Luke 23:34a, KJV). Do you realize that those words were for all of us? Take a minute and let that sink in. Jesus forgives you!

If this were not the case, then why did Jesus return to earth after presenting His blood to the Father? Why did He set Peter apart to have a private conversation and make sure that Peter knew he was forgiven? And then commission him to feed His sheep? Why did He speak to the two followers on the road to Emmaus and explain truth to them so that their eyes could be opened? Or why did He show doubting Thomas His hands?

Do you realize Jesus could have brought His blood to the altar of God, presented it, and then sat down without returning? He could have said, "Okay, I'm done! Let us hope that they figure out what we did and why we did it."

But Jesus went beyond even that, showing Himself to His disciples after His resurrection and telling them to wait for the Holy Spirit to anoint them. And the best, in my opinion, He saved for last. He stopped Saul on the road to Damascus, confronted him about persecuting the believers, changed his name, and then spent time teaching him the truth about grace!

If these incidences did not happen or were not true, then we might still be confused about Jesus' life and death, and we might have a reason to think He was angry. We might even look at Jesus as just a man or another prophet sent to Israel.

Jesus returned to His followers to show them how much He loved them, to clarify His message, and prove He was accepted by the Father. He also guaranteed that we would understand these truths by sending the Holy Spirit, who will remind us of what Jesus did and guide us in all truth. Jesus also used the transformation of Paul's understanding of Jesus portrayed in the scriptures to write about grace, forgiveness, the new covenant, and Jesus as our High Priest.

Does God Turn His Back on Those He Loves?

Some people believe that Jesus turns His back on us when we sin. That He does not hear your prayers or answer when we are in need. And I have to ask myself, "If God is the same today, yesterday, and forever, and Adam was the first to sin against God, then shouldn't God have turned His back on Adam and let him die in those sins?" But we know that is not what He did; God went looking for Adam and covered his sin.

I do believe, however, that we grieve the Spirit of God when we do not go to Him for direction and advice, when we are not moved by His promptings, when we do not study the scriptures to see Jesus, when we ignore Gods Word and choose to go our own way.

Notice these are all actions on our part. But this grieving also should show us how much we are loved and that it breaks God's heart when we are not walking in alignment with Him. Also, we should consider that God will do anything in His power to bring us into a healthy place. Remember, scripture tells us that it is the goodness of God that leads to repentance (Romans 2:4). He is the one who constantly shows mercy, faithfulness to Jesus' obedience, and forgiveness. He always does good towards us even when we have sinned against Him. While we were yet sinners, Christ died for us (Romans 5:8, NKJV).

Physical and Emotional Healing

Our healing was secured when Jesus took those stripes, those beatings, and died that death that we deserve. First Peter 2:24 (NJB) states, "He was bearing our faults in His own body on the cross, so that we might die to our own faults and live for holiness; through His wounds you have been healed."

And we read in Isaiah of the Messiah, Jesus. "But He was pierced for our transgressions, he was crushed for our iniquities; the punishment that brought us peace was on Him, and by his wounds we are healed" (Isaiah 53:5, NIV).

Physical and emotional healing does not come automatically. This is the work that Jesus did for us, but we must have a believing knowledge of that truth for ourselves. There are some keywords that we should understand if we are going to see the manifestation of healing in our lives. We have already looked at grace in a number of different ways, so let us explore some other important words: hope, faith, and belief.

When Jesus went to heaven, He sent His Holy Spirit to live in us just as He was alive in Jesus when He walked among us. With the Holy Spirit living in us comes the hope of the transformation from the inside out and the power to bring newness to our lives. The Holy Spirit brings the power to be healed, just as Jesus healed those on earth, by the power of His Spirit according to the Father's ways and timing so that He may get the glory.

Hope

The scripture tells us that hope does not put us to shame, "And hope does not put us to shame; because God's love has been poured out into our hearts through the Holy Spirit who has been given to us" (Romans 5:5, NIV). I believe that after grace comes hope. Hope is the confident expectation of the goodness of God. Notice that we are told it is an expectation; it is looking toward a future result.

Hope is when you see with your spiritual eyes what the Spirit is telling you, personally, for the situation you are in. It is based on the Word of God, but you have not experienced it in the natural realm as of yet. Hope is to anticipate, usually with pleasure and confidence, to expect and trust.

Hope is the confident expectation of the promises of God; it is based on God's faithfulness. When we invite God into a situation, the Holy Spirit will show us or remind us of the faithfulness of God. As we meditate on what has been revealed and on the faithfulness of God, it leads us into faith.

Hope it is not that "Aha" moment when you know for sure, that knowing deep inside you that what God has said has already been accomplished in heaven and is on its way into our natural world; that is what we call faith.

Hope keeps you looking forward. It causes you to seek God and stay close to Him. It should open your heart and mind to the truth of who Jesus is and how He wants to work in your life and the situation you are in.

Faith and Believing

Faith is also a gift from God, and it is the ability to have belief pull from the spiritual world what you need in the physical. Faith is the connecting power from the natural realm into the spiritual realm. Faith is part of the fruit of the Spirit. Jesus is the author and finisher of our faith. We all have faith growing in us. Jesus said that we only need faith that is the size of a mustard seed. And as we have discussed earlier, faith comes from hearing the word of God (Romans 10:17).

Faith and believing are not the same. Believing is our part; the more the Word gets into our hearts and minds, and we let the Spirit connect those truths with our spirit, the more we are able to believe what the truth of God's Word is saying to us as individuals and as a family or church.

The manifestation is God bringing it in His time into our reality. Faith shows itself through rest. If you want to know if you truly have faith, check your thought and prayer life. If you are not resting and praising from a sincere heart of gratitude, then you probably are still in the hope stage of the process. Ask God how to move from hope to faith. He will lead you to the truth. That is the Spirit's job, to lead us into all truth.

Howbeit when he, the Spirit of truth, is come, he will guide you into all truth; for he shall not speak of himself; but whatsoever he shall hear, that shall he speak: and he will shew you things to come. He shall glorify me: for he shall receive of mine, and shall shew it unto you. All things that the Father hath are mine: therefore said I, that he shall take of mine, and shall shew it unto you.

John 16:13–15 (KJV)

The beauty of how faith works in our lives is that it is the process of convincing us that what we expect from God will happen. When we have believed, it will cause an action to come forth. We will praise God, we will have boldness, we will be obedient to the promptings of the Spirit, or we will wait patiently, knowing that God will manifest what He has promised. The confident expectation will bring about faith, which then enables us to believe and have the patience to wait for the manifestation.

So many Christians beg God to do something; meanwhile, they think that asking is believing or that hoping that God will do something is the same as believing. I caught myself doing this. I found myself waiting for something to happen, watching the physical, thinking that I had faith. But faith believes the Word of God before it is seen. **"Now faith is the substance of things hoped for, the evidence of things not seen"** (Hebrews 11:1, KJV).

Do you want to know what the best thing I have learned these past eighteen months since Chip's hospitalization? God is faithful and true! Every time I have become disillusioned or discouraged, God has been faithful with a word, a verse, a teaching, or a song that has kept me hoping and increasing my ability to believe that His word is true. He is the author and finisher of our faith.

For example, I needed to understand how healing comes about, so the Lord led me to take classes on healing at Charis Bible College. Most of what I learned about healing was very new to me.

But what was not new to me was that I did have faith and that I believed God's Word above anything and everything. Another thing that needed to take place was my husband's understanding of how God views him. This is still a process that we are undergoing. I have been watching as God has been bringing passages of scriptures to us and revealing new insights.

I must admit I never knew the difference between faith and believing. I always thought they were the same. I know that the man asked Jesus to help his unbelief, but I did not really know how the two differed.

So, I can honestly say that I am still in the process of understanding healing and the finished work of Christ, but I am confident that He who has begun an excellent work in me and in my husband will carry it on to completion until the day of Christ Jesus.

God is so wonderful. My husband had the flu this past weekend. On Monday night, we listened to a teaching on what we have inside us because of Jesus' finished work. After watching the program, my husband asked me a question, "Were the people who were healed and mentioned on the program still healed?"

I was able to say yes because I had heard testimonies directly from them while taking classes or watching other programs that had aired. The next day Chip stayed home from work but was much better. Not only did he work from home, but we went to a few stores, did errands, and purchased Italian submarine sandwiches for dinner.

While eating dinner, my granddaughter asked him if he had gone to work, and he replied no, but that he was feeling much better. He had prayed for healing the night before. *Wow!* This was the first time he had ever spoken of believing for healing for himself, claiming it through prayer and having the manifestation appear.

What is even more remarkable for me is that I had been praying and asking God what was stopping the manifestation of healing in my husband's life. The Lord had repeatedly spoken to me of his understanding of truth needing to be established.

The lesson we had heard the night before guaranteed us that God answers our prayers but that we have enemies, including doubt, that rob us of the manifestation. My husband took his first major step of true faith in God's healing power and saw God's Word of truth come forth from the spiritual to the natural.

CHAPTER 17

Back to the Pruning... The Second Branch

I believe that the second branch that needed to fall off was similar to the first, yet different. I am now realizing that the enemy keeps coming back and insisting that we need to produce more fruit, even if it is not time to do so.

In order for Jesus to do the will of His Father, He needed to spend time alone with Him in quietness and solitude. The fruit is in us; we have love, joy, peace, longsuffering, gentleness, goodness, faith, meekness, and temperance; against such, there is no law. But we are also told if we live in the Spirit, then we should walk in the Spirit (Galatians 5:22, 25, KJV). But if we are not walking in the Spirit, if we are going our own way, then His fruits will not come forth.

I was being pruned when I stopped listening to the voice that said, "Keep going; you do not need to rest."

There was an incredibly wise pastor who I had been under for several months during a leadership transition at our church. She also had walked through Chip's hospital visits and emails of prayer with us. And when ministry and activities started up again after the holidays, and I said I needed to stop and rest, she heard me. She refused to let me become part of anything extra.

Others were telling me to continue as I had done before the hospital visits, that I needed to show God's power through my actions, but she kept being an audible voice that said no. She stood in the gap for me, even when I did not know she was doing it. Her voice was gentle but affirmative, and it was what I needed. I was able to let go of some things that may have brought forth some benefits to me and the church eventually but were not where God was calling me at that time. And I was able to speak with her of things that I felt God had not prepared me for at the time but that others wanted to see me being a part of.

I have also come to see that the burden was lifted off of my shoulders; I was no longer carrying the weight of my ministry responsibilities. During those times when we say yes to rest, the Spirit of God refreshes us with gentle words of guidance and redirection. He comforts us in our distress, and He heals our wounds.

But I have to admit, this was a very awkward time as I watched people take my place in ministry, and I did not know if I would be cut down completely and tossed away. But my Gardener is kinder than that; He only throws into the fire that which would hurt us. And after a season of rest, just like my real apple tree did the following spring, I am sensing new blossoms growing in my heart, and my life is starting to feel refreshed. Our precious Gardener only cuts off what is harmful to us and keeps that which will benefit His kingdom, His children, and our world.

John 15:2 (NKJV) tells us Jesus said, "Every branch in Me that does not bear fruit, he takes away and every branch that does bear fruit he prunes, that it may bear more fruit." I am authoring this book in the space of my "nothingness" or, better yet, my "pruning" time. I am so glad that the True Vinedresser is much wiser than I am. I was pruned, not broken off. I still have fellowship with the Lord and with my spiritual family. As I stated in the last section, I am back in ministry, and my fruit is good; I feel the energy of God revitalizing me daily.

I went back into ministry a year later, but I do not feel the weight of trying to please people nor of taking on too many responsibilities with the expectation that I am responsible for them. I can let Jesus carry those loads now.

Drops

Are you aware that "drops," which are simply the fruit that drops to the ground before or during picking season, are still useful? Farmers use them to feed livestock, and the ones that are not picked up are mowed at the end of the season, and in doing so, they become fertilizer for next year's crop. As we lie dormant, when we die to self or do not try to be of use in our own strength and admit our sin or weaknesses, that is when the Holy Spirit is able to have His way in us, and we can become useful in the kingdom of God. So, do not be afraid to let others see your weaknesses or failures because you can still be used by God. God might just use you in an altogether unique way. My admitting that I needed to rest and to be healed actually spoke to people about taking time to rest and to hear God's voice themselves.

It Is a "God" Thing!

We sometimes wonder if God knows what He is doing, so let me share a few of what I call "it's a God thing" or, in other words, God's providence. One of the opportunities I had to let go of was a trip to Israel. I had found a roommate, secured a passport, and paid the initial down payment to secure our tickets and room, as well as the second payment due. This was a trip that I would be taking with our church and some of the pastors. I was extremely excited about the trip and all the traveling that we would be experiencing since I had never been out of the country. But as time went on, I felt uncomfortable about the trip. And as I prayed, the Lord told me that I would know whether to cancel the trip at my husband's next visit to his doctor for an ultrasound on his lungs.

My husband was rushed to the hospital before the scheduled date of that particular ultrasound would take place. And as I stood in the hallway of a major hospital in Boston waiting till my husband finished having a test done on his heart, the Lord reminded me of that conversation. I looked on my phone to see the date and realized it was the scheduled day for the ultrasound. I knew without a shadow of a doubt that I was not to go on the trip to Israel, and I immediately contacted our financial director. He told me not to worry about anything and that he would take care of it, which he did.

Because of the timing and of the deposits I had already paid into the agency, I received back the exact amount of money I needed to pay all my husband's medical bills and at the exact time that the bills were coming in. A few months later, the trip was canceled because of the coronavirus. But God, in His wisdom, knew I needed that money set aside for those bills, as well as my being home with my husband during the following weeks.

Another "God thing" was that one of the ministries that I would normally have had a role in planning and even leading a team for was canceled. I had been asked to join the team early in the planning stages and kept thinking it was not for me to be involved in this year, but it was one of those things that were weighing me down.

I stepped away, and it was one area that made me feel extremely uncomfortable, not being part of the planning team with my friends. I wanted so much to be involved, but I kept feeling as though I should not, and again it was the Holy Spirit whispering in my ear, "Not this year."

I have had a home bakery and have made the desserts in advance of the programs in the past years. And because I was able to listen, hear, and obey, even though at the time it had been hard, it saved me much. Our gathering was canceled due to the coronavirus. It would have cost me in time, effort, and finances. I would have baked all the desserts ahead of time, and it would have been a waste of product.

Thankfully, God in His goodness does not let us grow wildly on our own, as I did with my tree. He stepped in and showed me where I was going wild. He lovingly pruned me and healed those places that had been cut off. Pruning, watering, and fertilizing all must be a continuous part of the tree's maintenance, even after the tree has developed fruit. So, do not be ashamed when you need fertilizing.

Let God and people speak into your life. And when the pruning comes, it may seem painful at the time, but God knows what is best and only eliminates what is harmful to you or is dragging you down.

One beautiful part of this whole picture is that just like a tree will be familiar with its environment and will develop a regular routine of when to grow, when to produce, and when to rest, we, too, will learn the rhythm that God has for us, and we will flourish under His mighty hand.

Conclusion of This Chapter

I wrote the preceding chapters to show that the life that I now live, I live in Christ. And to show that God still speaks in dreams and visions, so if you think God has given you one, then go to Him and ask, "What might this mean?"

I wrote about the life of an apple tree to show that it is a progressive growth and that there are seasons. We cannot have good fruit until we are fully partnered with Christ. And that the enemy is always trying to rob, kill, or destroy, but our loving Heavenly Father knows how to take care of His own.

A few days after writing this chapter, the Lord impressed upon my heart a truth that I had not seen yet. In the first paragraphs of my writing, I tell the story of being chased and bullied by my friend. I mentioned that hurt people hurt people. And that when I was younger, I would hide until it was safe to come out and then run home. I knew I could not stand up against her taunts, her fists, and the gang that followed her.

But although I was wounded and very deeply hurt by another friend in the later section, the pruning of the tree, I did not run away. I stood and faced her several times. I challenged her and spoke truth to her as gently as I could. As I prayed before every meeting and repeatedly bent my knee to God's will and asked for His grace, God kept telling me in my spirit to ask for wisdom and for boldness. I had to pray earnestly for courage and that I would hear the voice of the True Lion of Judah over the voice of the lion that wanted to destroy me, which, by His grace, He gave me.

But I was also very aware that this friend was wounded, and when she felt the blows from others, she sent them my way. Up until this moment, I had not realized that I had come full circle. I did not hide; I did not leave the church, although I wanted to; I did not stop participating in ministry. I did not even stop being her friend. Right up until she left our church, I was there for her.

Instead, she asked for my forgiveness, and after a few conversations, I was able to forgive her. And although she has moved away, we still have a distant relationship. We still pray for each other and text each other.

God knows how to restore what the enemy has tried to destroy. I have also learned through this experience that God was pruning both of us and cutting off those branches of fear and cleansing those attitudes of insecurity in both of us.

It is not what is on the outside that God looks at, but it is the heart. Why do we do what we do, and to whom are we accountable?

Is our fruit genuinely good, or does it just look good on the outside but is not ripe on the inside?

We all walk along the path of life. And along the way, there is variety of trees or plants, and the Gardener knows what He is producing, how long it takes to produce it, and where He wants it to grow so that others can see the beauty of His love for us, or so that others can feed off the fruit that He produces.

Chapter 18

Standing on the Promises of God

Something I have learned along the way is that we need to learn how to stand on the promises of God. They will bring us such a sense of peace as we realize how faithful God is to His Word and to us.

Isaiah 55:10–11 tells us,

As the rain and the snow

come down from heaven,

and do not return to it

without watering the earth

and making it bud and flourish,

so that it yields seed for the sower and bread

for the eater,

so is my word that goes out from my mouth:

It will not return to me empty,

but will accomplish what I desire

and achieve the purpose for which I sent it.

Isaiah 55:10–11 (NIV)

If God has spoken a promise to you through His word, He will bring it about; it may not be in your timing or the way you might think it will happen, but it will come to pass. This is true of my salvation and of my being yielded to the lordship of Christ. In other words, I finally stopped doing things on my own and started to believe that if I trusted Jesus and listened to the Spirit, then I would know God's will and purpose for my life, and by His grace, I would be able to walk in it. We must also recognize that God has a perfect timing for everything.

God's Way and Timing Do Not Always Come About the Way We Think They Will

I remember a time when I was praying about our bills, and I believed God had told me that He was going to give us a large amount of money to help with our mortgage payments. I was so happy because I had already learned that He was faithful and true, so now I was able to hear Him and believe Him.

And so, I waited, and a few months later, again after praying about it, my husband and I were wondering if God was telling us to refinance our house. But God was at work, and we did not have to take matters into our own hands. The next week our bank called us to see if we wanted to refinance at a lower rate, and would not you know that at the time of our signing the papers, the banker told us that we had just reduced our mortgage payments by the exact amount God had put in my head. Now physically, I never saw the money, but my monthly payment decreased by over $500 dollars, and over the life of the loan, over $200,000. That was how God accomplished what His word was sent to do.

And what is so beautiful to me is the fact that God again knew what was going on in my heart and what my physical needs were going to be. Prior to this manifestation of God's goodness toward us were some difficult times and decisions that had to be made.

My dad had died a few months earlier. I had closed my business, which meant I was no longer surrounded with my daughters and grandchildren, who had worked with me and attended the day care. The friends I had made while watching their children had moved on to other schools. And when I tried to go back to Tuesday Bible study, my emotions were so raw that some comments that were made to me really hurt, and I stopped going.

Also, my brother was out of work, and since the day care was now closed, after my husband and I prayed about it, we had felt that we should hire him to repaint our house and fix some other areas that needed attending to. My husband is in construction and usually does all the work in our house, but we felt God had a reason for putting it on our hearts to hire my brother.

This took longer than we expected and cost us more than we had calculated at first. But we felt that the Lord was directing us to do so, and so out of obedience, we complied. By the time he was done working, our savings were incredibly low, and I had no new income coming in. My husband and I were concerned about how we would pay our mortgage. But God knows our needs and shows up with the answer at the correct time.

It took a few months of praying and waiting, but one day, our bank called us and told us that our credit was so good that they wanted to reduce our payments and lower our interest rate. Now, who does that? Really, a bank calling you. But it was true, and because of it, we were able to continue paying our bills and giving as we had been doing all along.

But even better than our financial gain was that while my brother was working, he heard my praise music going all the time, and we were able to have short conversations about grace and God's mercy. He started to ask more questions about how I lived and what I believed, then he started singing the songs with my CDs and started laughing and joking more around me and with me.

To my surprise, I received a phone call from his wife one day, and she said to me, "I do not know what happened at your house, but first he started singing, then he started praying again, and now we have started going back to church! Amen!"

God was doing a work in my brother's life while I was willing to give freely of my time, money, and testimony. And then God gave back to us by meeting our needs in such an unexpected way.

Do not ever be afraid to give freely when God puts it on your heart to do so. He always gives freely to us. But again, do we hear Him, and do we respond to that prompting?

Proverbs 23:4 tells us,

Do not weary yourself with getting rich, and have nothing to do with dishonest gain. You fix your gaze on this, and it is there no longer, for it is able to sprout wings like an eagle that flies off to the sky.

Proverbs 23:4 (TJB)

We are told to fix our eyes on Jesus, not on earthly things.

Waiting For the Right Time

God has an interesting way of bringing us into His goodwill. After having my day care for ten years, I wanted to get back into a Bible study. One of my mom's friends held a summer study with around thirty-five women who attended. So, I began to attend it.

Meanwhile, one Sunday, while the pastor was speaking at church, I heard that still small voice in my heart tell me I would be working in the kitchen. At the time, our church had recently opened a café and was looking for volunteers to help. So naturally, I thought this was where God was calling me to serve. But as I was leaving the balcony, where I sat regularly, I met someone, and we started talking. I forgot all about signing up to serve.

A few months later, the invitation was given again, but this time I had to leave the church in a hurry to get home to prepare for company coming later that day.

Then one day, while at the summer Bible study, the host asked one of my friends if she would help set up the coffee for the women's study at the church on Tuesday mornings. I quickly jumped in and said that I would help, thinking this is where God wants me to serve. The host told me no; she thought I lived too far away from the church and it would be too inconvenient to travel so far so early in the morning. So, a little confused and disappointed, I walked away from the conversation.

The next week the woman who had been asked to help approached me and asked if I would assist her. She felt she could not do it alone and loved our relationship and my energy. (I was a few years younger than she was.)

The next fall, we worked together as a team. But then she was called away to Texas because her daughter had cancer, and the doctors and treatment that she needed were there.

I took over the responsibility of the hospitality and invited a new friend to come to serve with me. We worked great together until the church closed due to COVID-19.

The amazing thing about this little act of obedience and waiting for God's timing was that it led me to not only do hospitality for the women's Bible study, but it also opened opportunities for my home bakery, catering jobs, funerals, and meetings at the church.

God Orchestrates Our Lives

Every year our women's ministries had two special events, women's Christmas event and a retreat for our women after the Christmas holidays. Both were well attended, and I had participated in both for several years. I loved both events and always invited my sister, my daughters, and my mom. We would get tables together or rooms together, and we would always help in whatever capacity they needed help. But I was never a lead person; I was always a behind-the-scenes person or a small-group facilitator.

But one year, I felt the Lord tell me that I was to participate in the next women's Christmas event. The only thing was, I was not invited by the pastor to attend the planning meeting. This is where God and His providence come in; just like in the story of Esther, God was in the background putting things together that I knew nothing about.

There was a Christian movie that was playing in a local theater, and my mom and I decided to go. We had been given tickets to see it and thought, why not! While at the movie, a woman from our church came over and started talking to me. She had been the lead coordinator of the Christmas event for the past years and had decided she could not do it any longer. There was a new pastor for women's ministry at our church, and my friend felt it was time for new people to step up into some of those positions. I had been on her team the year before as the registration coordinator, but it had been the first time that I had taken a role of such magnitude in this event.

As we were talking, she asked me if I was going to the meeting for the Christmas event. I told her no; I did not even know that there was to be one, and I had not been invited. She looked at me and said, "Well, you are now." She had been told she could bring one person that she thought would be willing and able to help.

I was her plus one. I went to the meeting knowing that I had not been invited by the pastor, but maybe God had a reason for the invite that was extended to me. During the meeting, people were asked what their spiritual gifts were and how God used them. Then we were asked if we were willing to step up into a position on the team. People stepped up for different positions, but no one stepped up to lead the group. After a few minutes, I half raised my hand. The pastor asked if there was anyone else willing to take on the role as coordinator, but no one else was willing. She asked again and again, but there was only one hand up, and it was mine. By default, I got the job.

As we left the meeting, the woman who had invited me stopped me in the parking lot and told me she knew that I was to have that position. This gave me a confidence that God was in the details and that He had been leading my steps and directing my paths. We had over five hundred women show up that year to our event, and it was beautiful! Lives were touched, and women were blessed. Jesus' name was lifted high!

Not Everything Is Smooth Sailing

Of course, there are always lessons that we need to learn along the way. This next lesson I want to share I luckily learned early in my walk with God. In Galatians 3:28 (KJV), it states, "There is neither Jew nor Greek, there is neither bond nor free, there is neither male nor female: for ye are all one in Christ Jesus."

This verse was new to my way of thinking when I was young. It became a verse that I had to wrestle over. It happened when I was leading my second team for our VBS program. In my first leadership role, I was a craft coordinator for our VBS program. I had all women on my team. After seven years of leading the craft team, I was asked to take on a larger role in the recreation program of VBS.

I had heard the whisper of God telling me that I would be the coordinator for the "Wreck" team during our VBS, and in the first year, I took on the role as the leader. It was in the second year that the problems took place because I allowed a false pattern of thinking to rule my life rather than the role God had called me to. I foolishly took on the role of following, not leading.

The following year after the Spirit had whispered to me, I was asked to lead the team. I had been anticipating the ask since I had learned to hear God's whisper and to wait for the invite. The first year went very well. But in the second year of my leading the team, I was given an assistant who was a man. I did not understand my role and let him make decisions that were harmful to our team. For a point of reference, our team consisted of about thirty-five people, including teenagers and adults.

By the end of the week, I had people mad at me. Parents were threatening to not let their teens come back the following year, and I was devasted. I had let my team down, and I had not been the leader that God had called me to be. I was listening to man and not to the Spirit who leads and directs.

I was so ashamed that I felt I could no longer lead a team, and I was considering telling the pastor I would not be back the following year. But as I was drowning in self-pity, my dear friend, the Holy Spirit, showed up. He dried my tears, squared up my shoulders, and gave me insights that I had not seen before. He reminded me that He had called me to lead the group, not the person I had given my authority to. He showed me that there is no male and female in His kingdom work but that we are all called according to His purposes. He had a purpose for me to lead the team, and He had a plan as to how to move forward.

A few days later, our pastor of Children's Christian Education called me into his office, and we had a conversation that blew me away. I thought he was going to tell me that he had chosen someone else to lead the team the next year, but instead, he started to talk to me about the following year and what ideas I had about moving forward. Everything that the Lord had spoken to me the last few days, He had spoken to this pastor also, and we were in complete agreement. My assistant was asked to step down, and someone else came on my team to partner with me. But this time, when we were not in agreement as to how something should be handled, I took the lead, and my voice was heard.

We had seven years working together, and the Spirit was leading the team, and we had lots of fun together. My team stayed together, and there were no more incidents that led to pain or grief. God knows how to give beauty for ashes and change shame into glory!

"being confident of this, that he who began a good work in you will carry it on to completion until the day of Christ Jesus"
(Philippians 1:6, NIV).

The wonderful truth is that with God and in step with God does not guarantee smooth sailing, but He does promise to work it out for good.

> *"And we know that all things work together for good to those who love God, to those who are the called according to His purpose"* *(Romans 8:28, NKJV).*

CHAPTER 19

The Clock!

The last dream or vision I want to speak about happened also when I was incredibly young in my walk with Jesus. I remember seeing a clock on a tower, it was exceptionally large, and it was round. The numbers were bold and raised from the face of the clock. The hands also were quite noticeable and were both reaching toward twelve. When I asked what the clock represented, I was told that time was short. Now, this was forty years ago, but even back then, there was a sense of urgency when I viewed the clock.

God Wants Us to Use Our Time Wisely by Bringing the Good News of Salvation to the Lost World

Once we are saved from this fallen world and the sin that so easily trips us up, we are new creations in Christ. Second Corinthians 5:17 (KJV) states, "Therefore if any man be in Christ, he is a new creature: old things are passed away; behold, all things are become new."

Because we are now a new creation, the Spirit of God dwells in us and gives us gifts to build each other up, to grow us into maturity, and to bring the Good News of salvation to the world. Each of us has a different gift or gifts given to us by the Spirit of God. Without these gifts, we would not be able to accomplish what God has called us to do to further His kingdom.

What Are Our Spiritual Gifts?

What are the gifts, and where do we find them in the Bible?

In Romans 12:6–11, we find,

Our gifts differ according to the grace given us. If your gift is *prophecy*, use it as your faith suggests; if *administration*, then use it for administration; if *teaching*, use it for teaching. Let the *preachers* deliver sermons, the *almsgivers* give freely, the *officials* be diligent, and those who do works of *mercy* do them cheerfully. Do not let your love be a pretense, but sincerely prefer good to evil. Love each other much as brothers should and have a profound respect for each other.

Romans 12:6–11 (TJB)

There is a variety of gifts but always the same Spirit; there are all sorts of service to be done, but always to the same Lord; working in all sorts of different ways in different people, it is the same God that is working in all of them. The particular way that the Spirit is given to each person is for a good purpose. One may have the gift of *preaching with wisdom* given him by the Spirit; another may have the gift of *preaching instruction* by the same Spirit; and another the gift of *faith* given by the same Spirit; another the gift of *healing*, through this one Spirit; one the *power of miracles*; another *prophecy*; another the gift of *recognizing spirits*; another the gift of *tongues* and another the *ability to interpret them*. All these are the work of one and the same Spirit, who distributes gifts to different people just as He chooses.

1 Corinthians 12:4–11 (TJB)

And to some, His gift was that they should be *apostles*; to some *prophets*; to some *evangelists*; to some *pastors* and *teachers*; so that the saints together make a unity in the work of service, building up the body of Christ. In this way we are all to come to unity in our faith and in our knowledge of the Son of God, until we become the perfect Man, fully matured with the fullness of Christ Himself.

Ephesians 4:11–13 (TJB)

Everything will soon come to an end, so, to pray better keep a calm and sober mind. Above all, never let your love for each other grow insincere, since love covers many sins. *Welcome each other into your houses* without grumbling. Each one of you has received a special grace, so, like *good stewards* responsible for all these different graces of God, put yourselves at the *service of others*. If you are a *speaker*, speak in words that seem to come from God; if you are a *helper*, help as though every action was done at God's

orders; so that in everything God may receive glory, through Jesus Christ, since to Him alone belong all the glory and power forever and ever. Amen.

1 Peter 4:7–11 (TJB)

God the Father has thought of our every need and has put the responsibility on all of us to do our part. But He has never asked us to do it in our own strength or ability. It is always through the working of the Spirit in our lives and by grace and faith working together. God's part is grace; our part is faith: believing what Jesus has done and the promises God has given to His church.

There is one more important truth to add here. It is that nothing is done by faith without grace.

Grace shows us the provisions that Jesus has purchased for us in His sacrifice on the cross, being extended to us in a variety of ways: one is His unconditional love for us, another is the divine influence upon our heart and its reflection in our lives, including gratitude, being accepted, benefits, favor, gifts, joy, liberality, and pleasure.

Faith is our believing in what He has done and the promises given to us. Ephesians 2:8–9 (KJV) tells us, "For by grace are ye saved through faith; and that not of yourselves: it is the gift of God: Not of works, lest any man should boast."

We need to see and understand that everything that we are believing for has already been provided through grace; it is a gift from God. It is not from something that we do or earn. It is provided by what Jesus has done for us. We cannot believe for something that

God has not already provided. But once we understand who and what we are in Christ Jesus and what He has provided, then we can ask and believe for it.

I became acutely aware of the truth of healing when I started to believe that healing is a part of our atonement. I love that in both the New Testament and Old Testament, we are told that by Jesus' stripes, we are healed.

Isaiah 53:5 (KJV) states, "But he was wounded for our transgressions, he was bruised for our iniquities; the chastisement for our peace was upon him, and by his stripes we are healed." The word *"healed"* used here is the word *"raphah"* in Hebrew; it means to mend (by stitching), to cure, (cause to) heal, physician, repair, x thoroughly, make whole.

First Peter 2:24 (NKJV) tells us, "who Himself bore our sins in His own body on the tree, that we, having died to sins, might live for righteousness—by whose stripes you were healed." The word for *"heal"* in this verse is *"iaomai,"* which means to cure (lit or fig), heal, make whole.

I love that Jesus loved me so much that He took the beatings that I deserve so that I could be healed. Some people today believe that God only heals people emotionally or spiritually in our times. But I disagree.

Do you realize that the word "salvation" in Greek is "soteria," meaning rescue or safety (phys. or mor.): deliver, health, salvation, save, saving?

I do not have the gift of healing as some may have, but I do have the gift of faith, and I do believe what those two verses are saying to me. I also know that I have the same Spirit that raised Jesus from the dead living in me.

I cannot help but think of Abraham: in the natural realm, he and Sarah should not have been able to bear a child. But through faith, they inherited the promise. He believed God and was considered righteous.

So, once I started to believe what was given to me by grace, I was able to access and receive healing.

One instance was when I had a fever and several other symptoms for about three days. I quarantined myself from my family members and only left the room when no one was home. On the third day, I sensed in my spirit to pray for healing and to command the infection to leave my body. Within an hour, I was symptom-free.

Another time, I had an eye infection, and my cheek swelled up. Again, I prayed, believing that I was not under the curse and that Jesus had paid for my sin and sickness and that I did not want Him to have paid in vain. I immediately felt the sting and itching go away, but it was a few hours before the swelling went down. But by dinner time, I was able to look in the mirror and see that my face was back to normal.

I am not saying that I do not get sick, but I do know who to go to and how to speak to the illness when it tries to attack my body.

Jesus Did Only What He Saw the Father Do

I was listening to a pastor the other day who spoke of Jesus only doing what He saw the Father do. John 5:19 tells us,

Then Jesus answered and said to them, "Most assuredly, I say to you, the Son can do nothing of Himself, but what He sees the

Father do; for whatever He does, the Son also does in like manner."

John 5:19 (NKJV)

What the pastor was saying was that even Jesus listened to the Spirit and was led by God to learn who He was to heal or impart a miracle for and how. Notice the verse tells us that Jesus can do nothing of Himself but only what He sees the Father do. Jesus and the Spirit are one with the Father. Therefore, He will never go against the Father because He cannot!

How did Jesus see what the Father was doing? The Father was not on earth physically performing miracles, feeding people, or even teaching. No, Jesus saw the Father's will through His Spirit, just the same as we do. This should be overly exciting to us. Jesus came to show us that through the power of the Holy Spirit of God living in us, we can do the same works that Jesus did. Why? Because He was doing it through the same power that lives in us as His children. "Verily, verily, I say unto you, He that believeth on me, the works that I do shall he do also; and greater works than these shall he do; because I go unto my Father" (John 14:12, KJV).

Jesus was directed by His Father and led by the Spirit; He was empowered by the Spirit to bring glory and honor to the Father. We are not to be running around doing our own thing and then sticking God's name to it.

True power comes from God and God alone. It is manifested when we hear or read the Word of God, and we believe what He is telling us; then, in obedience, we walk in that truth, and we leave the results and timing to God.

When we believe God, we will have the ability to rest, to wait patiently for God to fulfill His promises and purposes for His glory.

What Are You Doing with Your Talents?

So do not be afraid to use your gifts, even if they are a little unorthodox to your local church. Jesus will be returning soon, and Father God will ask about what we did with the gifts that He gave us to use to build up His church. I cannot help but think of the servant who hid his talents.

"For the kingdom of heaven is like a man traveling to a far country, who called his own servants and delivered his goods to them. And to one he gave five talents, to another two, and to another one, to each according to his own ability; and immediately he went on a journey. Then he who received the five talents went and traded with them and made another five talents. And likewise, he who had received two gained two more also. But he who received one went and dug in the ground and hid his lord's money. After a long time, the lord of those servants came and settled accounts with them.

"So, he who had received five talents came

and brought five other talents, saying, 'Lord, you delivered to me five talents; look, I have gained five more talents besides them.' His lord said to him, 'Well done, good and faithful servant; you were faithful over a few things; I will make you ruler over many things. Enter into the joy of your lord.' He also who had received two talents came and said, 'Lord, you delivered to me two talents; look, I have gained two more talents besides them. His lord said to him, 'Well done, good and faithful servant; you have been faithful over a few things, I will make you ruler over many things. Enter into the joy of your lord.'

"Then he who had received the one talent came and said, 'Lord, I knew you to be a hard man, reaping where you have not sown, and gathering where you have not scattered seed. And I was afraid and went and hid your talents in the ground. Look, there you have what is yours.'

"But his lord answered and said to him, 'You wicked and lazy servant, you knew that I reap where I have not sown and gather where I have not scattered seed. So you ought to have deposited my money with the bankers, and at my coming I would have received back my own with interest. So take the talent from him, and give it to him who has ten talents. 'For to everyone who has, more will be given, and he will have abundance; but from him who does not have, even what he has will be taken away. And cast the unprofitable servant into the outer darkness. There will be weeping and gnashing of teeth.'"

Matthew 25:14–30 (NKJV)

Power Thoughts to the Parable

The first thing to notice is that the Lord gave talents both to those who would be trustworthy with the gifts and to him who would not be. And notice that He did not give all of them the same number of talents. The amount was based on their abilities, an individual amount for each servant, but they were given the same opportunity, or better said, the same time to use them. He did not return for a long while, giving ample time for the servants to invest and increase the talents.

> We should be asking ourselves: how are we using the gifts that have been imparted to us by the Spirit?

> Second, we see the thinking behind each of the servants; the first two servants wanted to please the lord, so in response, they found a way to invest the talents. And in doing so, they saw an increase that they could give back to the lord. The servant who only had one talent thought he did not have to do anything because he could not understand how or why the lord did the things that he did, and so he hid his talents and did not increase them.

> Is Jesus Lord of your life? Are you looking forward to His return, or are you being lazy, thinking you do not have to do anything because God is going to do what He wants when He wants?

> Some people believe this is what sovereignty means: they excuse themselves from the equation and think that God is responsible for everything, like a puppet master pulling all the strings, not expecting them to do anything on their own. But we have been given free will, and we get to choose if we will honor God with our lives and work with the Spirit to do the kingdom work that Jesus started or not.

> Do you see God as a hard man whom you fear? Do you find

it hard to trust that He has provided, through Jesus, all that you need for life and salvation? The man who buried his talents did not know the lord personally as a friend. Jesus wants a personal, loving relationship with us.

➤ And although we are servants, He does not treat us as so. John 15:15–17 states,

No longer do I call you servants, for a servant does not know what his master is doing; but I have called you friends, for all things that I heard from My Father I have made known to you. You did not choose Me, but I chose you and appointed you that you should go and bear fruit, and that your fruit should remain, that whatever you ask the Father in My name He may give you. These things I command you, that you love one another.

John 15:15–17 (NKJV)

Once we receive salvation by grace through faith, we are given the Holy Spirit, and He tells us all things that we need to know if we will ask Him. This wicked and lazy servant did not ask what the lord wanted him to do with the talent; he made his own decisions and choices based on his opinion of the lord.

The third thing to notice is the lord's expectation of his servants: he expected them to invest, to take risks, to go out to the marketplace to find a way to increase what he had given them. He was pleased with the first two, not because of the return but because of their investment, initiative, and faithfulness. It showed their hearts' motivation and their desire to increase the lord's wealth.

But what about the servant who hid the talents? He did not have the correct view of the master; that servant viewed the lord as a hard taskmaster. Let us stop right here and realize that the Law is the hard taskmaster as well as the enemy of our soul.

Jesus is loving and kind, gentle and long-suffering. And yes, we have to admit we do not always understand His working or His ways. But, with that in mind, we do not have to fear Him but instead be grateful that we have been invited to be a part of His mission.

Finally, notice the rewards: the servants who invested their talents were both praised and went from investors to rulers. We, too, go from servant to ruler and have the joy of the Lord, which is our strength!

Yet, the lazy servant is not welcome into the kingdom; he loses what was given to him, and he is thrown into outer darkness. This is an incredibly sad and somber thought, and it takes me back to the beginning of my life. I was afraid of God because I did not know the truth of who He was and how He viewed me.

But unlike the wicked and lazy servant, the Spirit in me was wooing me back to God. Every chance I had, I prayed and asked for deliverance from my hurts, my addictions, and my actions. And Jesus, Himself, forgave me and brought me into the experiential knowledge that He was in my heart and had been since I asked Him in as a child.

Again, the beauty of Jesus is that He told us that He would not leave us but would send His Spirit, and it is His Spirit that brings understanding of what Jesus accomplished on the cross for us and gives us the talents to use for His kingdom.

➤ So, have you come to know the Lord? Are you taking the talents that the Spirit has given you and using them for the building of the kingdom? Do you see the Lord as a hard man or as the Lord who praises and rewards faithfulness?

Chapter 20

The Conclusion to the Matter!

Jesus is the author and finisher of your faith. He was there before you even went looking for Him, and He will be there when you take your last breath.

He wants to have a growing, vibrant relationship with you, and He knows how to help you mature.

God speaks to us through the scriptures (the Bible), through songs, through other people, through the Spirit (through our thoughts). He can speak through anything He wants, including a donkey! Just make sure it is Him speaking.

We are transformed by the renewing of our minds as we study God's Word and ask hard questions.

It is not enough to just hear the Word, but we must be doing what it says or what the Spirit is prompting us to do.

Having friends who are on the same path as us will help us to grow and become stronger in our faith.

Fear does not have to be part of our mindset because God has already ordained your steps, and He knows how to get you where you are supposed to go, even if there seem to be detours along the way.

Unfortunately, we do feel pain along the way, but that does not mean that God hates you or has rejected you. It means that the enemy is out to get you, sidetrack you, rob, or steal from you.

Sometimes God does allow situations in our lives that are most uncomfortable for us because He wants to show Himself larger than the enemy's attack. And when we keep our eyes on Jesus, He will see us through to the end, He will rescue us when we need it, He will bind up our wounds, He will prevent us from falling or going in the wrong direction, and He will fill us with unimaginable joy.

And most of all—give yourself time to grow and do not compare yourself to others. They have their own journey to walk and their own burdens to carry.

So...

> If you have struggled with sin in your life, go to Jesus.

> He is the God who forgives... "El Nose" comes from the verb to lift, carry, or take. God takes our sins away and carries our burdens.

> He heals... He is Jehovah-Rapha: the God who heals.

> He can give you a new beginning; He gave me one.

> If you are not sure if you have ever heard the Spirit, ask Jesus to make it clear. "The Spirit himself testifies with our spirit that we are children of God" (Romans 8:16, NIV).

> If you cannot forgive yourself or someone else, remember Jesus has, and He will also enable you.

> If you cannot understand what the Bible is saying to you, talk to someone who knows Jesus.

When I was younger, I did not understand what was so big about Jesus. I did not understand the relevance of the Bible stories, and I did not see how they fit into our daily lives. But the truth is, you never really live life until you do it with Jesus. And the stories of the Bible are to show us how God intervened in regular people's everyday, ordinary lives and how Jesus came to give us life and to give it to us abundantly.

We look at the people of faith in the Bible and see them as giants, but they were just living ordinary lives on an extraordinary journey. What made them giants was their belief in God's Word to them personally and how moved they were by it.

So, take a look at your life; it may be as simple as mine is, you may not feel that you have any significance to share with others, but if you have let Jesus be Lord, you will also have stories to tell and people to influence.

And most of all, enjoy the journey! ...God's got you; it was His plan all along!

"'For I know the plans I have for you,' declares the LORD, 'plans to prosper you and not to harm you, plans to give you hope and a future'" (Jeremiah 29:11, NIV).

About the Author

CJ Cutaia has been married to her husband, Charles, for the past forty-three years. She has four children and seven grandchildren.

She lives in Massachusetts, where she attends and serves as a small group Bible study leader and a greeter at her local church.

Endnotes

1.   Strong's Concordance
2.   Strong's Concordance
3.   Strong's Concordance
4.   Strong's Concordance

CPSIA information can be obtained
at www.ICGtesting.com
Printed in the USA
BVHW090358060722
641300BV00010B/950